CALEB ROSS

High Performance Computing With C#10 And .NET 6

First edition

This book was professionally typeset on Reedsy.
Find out more at reedsy.com

Contents

Introduction   1

Chapter 1: Introduction to High-Performance Computing (HPC)   8

Chapter 2: The Evolution of .NET and C# for Performance   18

Chapter 3: Memory Management and Optimization in
.NET 6   28

Chapter 4: Asynchronous Programming for Performance   39

Chapter 5: Multithreading and Parallel Programming   50

Chapter 6: Task-Based Asynchronous Programming with TPL   66

Chapter 7: Performance Testing and Benchmarking in
.NET 6   89

Chapter 8: Memory Management and Optimization Techniques in...   100

Chapter 9: Advanced Performance Optimization Techniques in...   114

Chapter 10: Building Scalable Applications with .NET 6   128

Chapter 11: Security Considerations in High-Performance...   139

Chapter 12: Monitoring and Maintaining High-Performance...   149

Chapter 13: Leveraging Cloud Services for Scalability and... 160

Chapter 14: Ensuring Data Security and Compliance in
.NET 6...   171

Chapter 15: Best Practices for Deploying High-Performance... 182

Conclusion: Mastering High-Performance Applications with...   194

Introduction

Importance of High-Performance Computing (HPC) in Modern Software Development

High-Performance Computing (HPC) has become an integral aspect of modern software development, influencing a vast array of industries. It serves as the driving force behind innovations in fields such as artificial intelligence (AI), machine learning (ML), financial modeling, scientific simulations, and big data analytics. In an age where data generation and processing have reached unprecedented scales, the demand for systems that can efficiently handle these tasks has skyrocketed. This is where HPC steps in, providing the necessary computational power to meet these demands.

HPC refers to the use of parallel processing techniques to perform large-scale computations at high speeds. It typically involves the use of supercomputers or clusters of computers working in concert to process massive amounts of data or execute complex algorithms. In contrast to traditional computing, which handles tasks sequentially, HPC allows for the simultaneous execution of tasks, significantly reducing processing time and enabling solutions that would otherwise be unattainable.

In the context of modern software development, HPC enables developers to create applications that perform complex calculations, process big data in real-time, and simulate intricate systems across various domains. For instance, financial institutions rely on HPC for real-time trading algorithms and risk

1

assessments, while the healthcare sector uses it for bioinformatics, drug discovery, and genomics research. Similarly, weather forecasting, aerospace, and automotive industries depend on HPC for simulations that require precise and intensive calculations.

1. **The Role of HPC in Industry: Industries such as finance, energy, and pharmaceuticals rely on HPC for risk management, predictive analytics, and modeling. For example, financial firms run models to predict market trends, energy companies use it for complex simulations in oil exploration, and pharmaceutical companies depend on HPC for drug development. The applications of HPC extend beyond these industries into areas like film production for rendering graphics, autonomous vehicles for sensor data processing, and even space exploration, where HPC assists in handling vast amounts of data from satellite sensors.

2. **Complex Problems and Efficient Solutions: One of the core reasons for HPC's growing relevance in software development is its ability to solve computationally intensive problems that were once impractical due to hardware limitations. Software developers can now design solutions that involve data sets containing billions of records, execute sophisticated models, and simulate processes with thousands of variables. As a result, these solutions are pushing the boundaries of what's possible in technology.

3. **Reduced Time to Insight: For businesses, time is a crucial resource. The faster an organization can gain insights from data, the more competitive it becomes. HPC enables businesses to process data quickly, gain insights faster, and make real-time decisions that drive growth. In financial markets, for instance, algorithms that can process and react to new information in milliseconds are a distinct advantage, and HPC provides the computational resources necessary to achieve this level of speed.

4. **Enhanced Computational Power: HPC delivers not only speed but also power. It can handle vast volumes of data and process millions of transactions per second, making it ideal for industries such as telecommunications, e-commerce, and finance. For example, HPC systems enable real-time fraud detection by processing large data sets and running sophisticated algorithms that identify suspicious activities before damage is done.

5. Energy Efficiency and Cost-Effectiveness: HPC is also paving the way for energy-efficient computing. With advancements in hardware and software, modern HPC systems are being designed to perform computationally intensive tasks while consuming less energy than previous generations. This results in cost savings for businesses that rely heavily on large-scale data processing and simulation.

Why C# 10 and .NET 6 for HPC

When discussing programming languages and frameworks suited for high-performance computing, C# 10 and .NET 6 are not the first technologies that typically come to mind. Historically, languages like C, C++, and Fortran have dominated the HPC landscape, thanks to their low-level memory control and ability to optimize hardware utilization. However, C# 10 and .NET 6 have emerged as formidable contenders in the HPC space due to their ongoing improvements in performance, multi-platform capabilities, and modern language features.

1. Performance Improvements: .NET 6, in particular, has made significant strides in terms of performance. The runtime has been optimized to handle memory management more efficiently, reduce the overhead associated with garbage collection, and improve startup times. Furthermore, the Just-In-Time (JIT) compiler has been enhanced to better optimize code for execution. This means that C# applications running on .NET 6 can now approach the performance levels of traditionally low-level languages, making them viable for high-performance applications.

2. Multi-threading and Asynchronous Programming: One of the key reasons for C# 10's suitability in HPC is its robust support for multi-threading and asynchronous programming. In any high-performance environment, the ability to break tasks down into parallel threads is crucial for optimizing resource usage and reducing processing times. C# offers tools like the Task Parallel Library (TPL) and the async/await model, which simplify the process of writing concurrent and parallel code.

The new language features in C# 10, such as record structs and enhanced pattern matching, further optimize the language for performance-critical applications. Developers can now write code that minimizes heap allocations,

3

improves memory access patterns, and leverages modern CPU architectures more effectively. These improvements make C# a strong contender in the HPC space, particularly for applications that require high throughput and low latency.

3. Cross-Platform Capabilities: One of the game-changing features of .NET 6 is its cross-platform nature. With .NET Core, Microsoft embraced the idea of multi-platform compatibility, allowing developers to write applications that run on Windows, Linux, and macOS. This flexibility is particularly beneficial in the context of HPC, where different platforms may be used to run various parts of a distributed computing system. For instance, a Windows-based development environment may be used to create applications that are ultimately deployed on Linux-based HPC clusters.

The cross-platform nature of .NET 6 also extends to cloud environments, which are becoming increasingly important for HPC. Cloud providers like Microsoft Azure, Amazon Web Services (AWS), and Google Cloud Platform (GCP) offer scalable, on-demand computing resources that are perfect for HPC tasks. With .NET 6, developers can build HPC applications that run seamlessly in these cloud environments, leveraging the massive computational power available in the cloud while maintaining the flexibility to run on different platforms.

4. Ease of Use and Developer Productivity: C# has always been known for its ease of use and developer productivity. With its modern syntax, rich library ecosystem, and integrated development environment (IDE) support (especially in Visual Studio), C# allows developers to write high-performance code without sacrificing readability and maintainability. The language's object-oriented nature, combined with functional programming features, provides a flexible and powerful development experience that encourages best practices in code organization, modularity, and reusability.

Moreover, .NET 6 includes a variety of libraries and frameworks that make it easier to integrate HPC capabilities into C# applications. For instance, libraries like PLINQ (Parallel LINQ) allow developers to implement parallel processing in a declarative way, making it simpler to optimize data processing tasks without writing low-level code. The ecosystem also includes specialized

4

libraries for scientific computing, machine learning, and data processing, all of which contribute to C# and .NET 6's suitability for HPC.

5. **Community and Ecosystem Support: The C# and .NET community is one of the largest and most active in the world. This means that developers working on HPC applications in C# and .NET have access to a wealth of resources, including tutorials, documentation, open-source projects, and forums where they can ask questions and seek advice. Furthermore, Microsoft's commitment to open-source development ensures that the .NET ecosystem continues to grow and evolve, incorporating new features and optimizations over time.

Overview of the Book Structure and Key Concepts

This book is structured to provide a comprehensive guide to implementing high-performance computing solutions using C# 10 and .NET 6. It begins by introducing readers to the foundational concepts of HPC and explaining why C# and .NET 6 are suitable technologies for this domain. From there, the book delves into performance optimization techniques, parallel programming, memory management, and data access, providing practical examples and case studies along the way.

Chapter 1: Introduction to HPC – This chapter covers the basic principles of high-performance computing, its history, and its current applications across various industries. It introduces readers to key concepts like parallelism, distributed computing, and the role of hardware in HPC.

Chapter 2: The Evolution of .NET for Performance – In this chapter, readers will explore the evolution of the .NET framework, focusing on the performance improvements introduced in .NET 6. It provides an overview of how .NET has become a viable platform for HPC applications and compares its performance to other frameworks and languages traditionally used in HPC.

Chapter 3: Memory Management and Optimization – This chapter focuses on memory management in .NET 6, including techniques for reducing memory consumption, optimizing garbage collection, and handling large data sets more efficiently. It also covers advanced topics like Span<T> and Memory<T> for high-performance applications.

Chapter 4: Asynchronous Programming – This chapter explains the importance of asynchronous programming in HPC applications, detailing how C# 10's async/await model can be used to optimize I/O-bound tasks and improve the overall performance of applications.

Chapter 5: Multithreading and Parallelism – In this chapter, readers will learn about multithreading and parallelism in C#, including the Task Parallel Library (TPL) and Parallel LINQ (PLINQ). It covers strategies for breaking tasks into parallel threads and optimizing resource usage.

Chapter 6: Advanced Techniques for Task Parallelism – This chapter dives deeper into task parallelism, covering advanced topics like custom task schedulers, handling concurrency with locks, and optimizing parallel loops for performance.

Chapter 7: Performance Testing and Benchmarking – This chapter teaches readers how to measure the performance of their applications using tools like BenchmarkDotNet. It provides guidelines for setting up benchmarks, interpreting performance results, and identifying bottlenecks in code.

Chapter 8: Cross-Platform HPC with .NET 6 – This chapter explores the cross-platform capabilities of .NET 6 and provides practical examples of building HPC applications that run on Windows, Linux, and macOS.

Chapter 9: HPC in Cloud Environments – This chapter discusses how to deploy HPC applications to cloud platforms like Azure, AWS, and GCP. It covers the benefits of using cloud-based HPC resources and provides best practices for optimizing performance in cloud environments.

Chapter 10: Optimizing Data Access – In this chapter, readers will learn how to optimize data access in C# 10 applications, focusing on efficient use of LINQ, PLINQ, and asynchronous data streams.

Chapter 11: HPC and Machine Learning – This chapter explains how HPC techniques can be applied to machine learning workflows using ML.NET and other .NET libraries. It provides practical examples of building high-performance AI models and optimizing data processing pipelines.

Chapter 12: Code Optimization Techniques – In this chapter, readers will explore advanced code optimization techniques, including low-level optimizations like SIMD, vectorization, and minimizing CPU bottlenecks.

Chapter 13: Real-World Case Studies – This chapter presents real-world case studies of HPC applications in industries like finance, healthcare, and scientific research. Each case study illustrates how C# and .NET 6 can be used to solve complex computational problems.

Chapter 14: Future Trends in HPC – This chapter looks at emerging trends in HPC, including quantum computing, edge computing, and other technologies that will shape the future of high-performance software development.

Chapter 15: Conclusion – The book concludes with a summary of the key takeaways and a discussion on the future potential of C# 10 and .NET 6 in the HPC space.

Chapter 1: Introduction to High-Performance Computing (HPC)

Defining HPC and Its Applications

H igh-Performance Computing (HPC) is a field of computing focused on the use of powerful hardware and sophisticated software to solve complex problems by performing large-scale computations at high speeds. It enables the simultaneous execution of multiple tasks, providing the computational power necessary to handle vast amounts of data and perform intensive calculations. HPC achieves this through parallel processing, leveraging multiple processors (or cores) to work on different parts of a task concurrently, significantly speeding up computation time compared to traditional sequential computing.

1. Parallel Processing as the Core of HPC At the heart of HPC is parallelism, which allows tasks to be divided into smaller sub-tasks that are executed simultaneously across different processors or nodes. This parallelism can be achieved at different levels, such as:

- **Data Parallelism**: Different chunks of a data set are processed simultaneously, reducing overall computation time.
- **Task Parallelism**: Independent tasks are performed in parallel, each on a separate processor, improving resource utilization.

- **Pipeline Parallelism**: Different stages of a process are executed in a pipelined fashion, where each stage processes different input simultaneously.

By combining these parallel techniques, HPC systems can achieve speeds several orders of magnitude greater than traditional computing systems, making it possible to tackle problems that would otherwise be intractable.

2. The Hardware Foundation of HPC The hardware used in HPC is typically more advanced than standard consumer-grade machines. Supercomputers, clusters of computers (also known as nodes), and specialized processors such as Graphics Processing Units (GPUs) are often employed. These systems are optimized for speed, memory access, and input/output (I/O) performance, allowing them to handle large-scale computations efficiently.

Key hardware components include:

- **Multi-core CPUs**: Central Processing Units (CPUs) with multiple cores that enable concurrent execution of instructions, essential for multi-threaded tasks.
- **GPUs**: Originally designed for rendering graphics, GPUs are now widely used in HPC for tasks like matrix computations, deep learning, and data processing. They provide massive parallelism, often with thousands of smaller cores capable of performing the same operation across different data sets.
- **High-Speed Networks**: HPC systems rely on high-speed, low-latency networks to facilitate communication between nodes in a cluster. Technologies such as InfiniBand or Ethernet are used to ensure that data transfer between nodes happens as quickly as possible.
- **Distributed Memory Systems**: HPC systems often employ distributed memory architectures, where each node in the system has its own memory that it can access independently. This reduces the bottlenecks associated with shared memory systems and allows the system to scale more efficiently.

9

**3. Software and Algorithms in HPC On the software side, HPC systems are powered by highly optimized algorithms that can make full use of the hardware's capabilities. These algorithms are designed to take advantage of parallelism, ensuring that tasks are split and distributed across processors effectively. In addition, HPC relies on specialized libraries and frameworks for parallel programming, such as:

- **MPI (Message Passing Interface)**: A standardized protocol used for communication between nodes in a distributed memory system. MPI allows different parts of a program to run on separate machines while communicating with each other as needed.
- **OpenMP (Open Multi-Processing)**: A framework that allows developers to write parallel code for multi-core CPUs. It simplifies the process of parallelizing existing programs by providing a set of directives that instruct the compiler on how to divide tasks between threads.
- **CUDA (Compute Unified Device Architecture)**: A parallel computing platform and programming model specifically designed for NVIDIA GPUs. CUDA allows developers to harness the computational power of GPUs for general-purpose computing tasks.

HPC in Different Industries

The applications of high-performance computing extend across a wide range of industries, each benefiting from its ability to process large volumes of data and perform complex calculations quickly. HPC is not limited to scientific research; it has become indispensable in industries like finance, healthcare, artificial intelligence, and even entertainment. The following sections highlight how different sectors rely on HPC to achieve breakthroughs in their fields.

1. HPC in Artificial Intelligence and Machine Learning

Artificial Intelligence (AI) and Machine Learning (ML) have grown exponentially in recent years, largely thanks to the computational power provided by HPC systems. Training AI models, especially deep learning models, requires massive amounts of data and computational resources. HPC systems, with their ability to parallelize tasks, make it feasible to train models on large datasets within a reasonable timeframe.

- **Deep Learning and Neural Networks**: Deep learning models, such as convolutional neural networks (CNNs) and recurrent neural networks (RNNs), involve billions of parameters and require substantial computational resources for training. HPC systems provide the necessary parallelism, allowing these models to be trained across thousands of GPUs simultaneously. This not only speeds up the training process but also enables the development of more complex models that can achieve higher accuracy.
- **Natural Language Processing (NLP)**: AI applications in natural language processing, such as language translation, sentiment analysis, and speech recognition, also benefit from HPC. By distributing tasks across multiple processors, HPC systems can process large text corpora or audio data efficiently, improving model performance and reducing the time needed for model inference.
- **Reinforcement Learning**: In reinforcement learning, agents learn by interacting with an environment, receiving feedback, and improving their behavior based on rewards or penalties. Simulating complex environments for reinforcement learning can be computationally expensive. HPC allows researchers to run multiple simulations in parallel, accelerating the learning process and enabling agents to learn more sophisticated behaviors.

2. HPC in Data Science and Big Data Analytics

Data science, which involves analyzing large datasets to extract valuable insights, has also seen significant advancements thanks to HPC. With the explosion of big data, traditional computing systems often struggle to process and analyze massive datasets in a timely manner. HPC systems, however, are built to handle such workloads, allowing data scientists to process and analyze data at scale.

- **Big Data Processing**: One of the primary challenges in data science is processing large datasets that may include millions or even billions of records. HPC systems excel at handling these datasets by using parallel processing to divide the data into smaller chunks and process them concurrently. Tools like Apache Hadoop and Apache Spark, when run on HPC clusters, can process vast amounts of data much faster than traditional systems.

- **Real-Time Analytics**: Many industries, such as finance and e-commerce, require real-time data analysis to make informed decisions. HPC systems enable the processing of data streams in real-time, allowing businesses to analyze data as it arrives and make decisions without delay. This is especially important in industries like stock trading, where milliseconds can make a difference in financial outcomes.

- **Predictive Modeling**: HPC is also essential for building predictive models, which involve processing historical data to make future predictions. These models are often computationally intensive and require substantial processing power to train. By using HPC systems, data scientists can train more accurate models in less time, enabling them to make more reliable predictions.

3. HPC in Financial Modeling

The finance industry relies heavily on high-performance computing for tasks like risk management, trading algorithms, and portfolio optimization. Financial models often involve complex mathematical calculations and large datasets, making HPC an essential tool for financial institutions.

- **Risk Management**: Financial institutions use HPC to perform risk assessments and manage their exposure to market fluctuations. By running simulations that account for various economic scenarios, financial analysts can assess the potential risks associated with different investments. These simulations often require complex calculations and large datasets, making HPC a crucial component of the risk management process.

- **Trading Algorithms**: High-frequency trading (HFT) algorithms are another area where HPC is indispensable. These algorithms rely on real-time data processing to make split-second trading decisions. HPC systems enable these algorithms to process vast amounts of financial data in real-time, allowing traders to capitalize on market opportunities before competitors can react.
- **Portfolio Optimization**: Portfolio optimization involves selecting the best mix of investments to achieve a desired return while minimizing risk. This requires solving complex mathematical models that take into account various factors like asset correlations, volatility, and market trends. HPC allows financial analysts to run these models more efficiently, enabling them to optimize portfolios more effectively.

4. HPC in Healthcare and Bioinformatics

The healthcare and life sciences industries have seen significant advancements thanks to HPC, particularly in areas like genomics, drug discovery, and medical imaging.

- **Genomics**: The analysis of genomic data involves processing large datasets that contain millions or billions of DNA sequences. HPC systems are used to perform tasks like DNA sequencing, genome assembly, and variant calling, which are essential for understanding the genetic basis of diseases and developing personalized treatments.
- **Drug Discovery**: The process of discovering new drugs involves running simulations that model the interactions between molecules and biological systems. These simulations are computationally intensive and require HPC to perform efficiently. By using HPC systems, researchers can accelerate the drug discovery process, reducing the time and cost required to bring new treatments to market.
- **Medical Imaging**: HPC is also used in medical imaging applications, such as MRI and CT scans. These imaging techniques generate large amounts of data that must be processed to create detailed images of the body's internal structures. HPC systems enable the rapid processing

of this data, allowing doctors to diagnose conditions more quickly and accurately.

5. HPC in Weather Forecasting and Climate Modeling

Weather forecasting and climate modeling are classic examples of applications that rely on HPC. These fields involve simulating complex systems that include interactions between the atmosphere, oceans, and land surfaces. The scale and complexity of these models make them ideal candidates for HPC.

- **Weather Forecasting**: HPC systems are used to run numerical weather prediction models that simulate the behavior of the atmosphere. These models require the processing of vast amounts of data, including satellite observations, radar data, and ground-based measurements. By using HPC, meteorologists can generate more accurate weather forecasts in less time, improving public safety and disaster preparedness.
- **Climate Modeling**: Climate models simulate the long-term behavior of the Earth's climate system, taking into account factors like greenhouse gas emissions, solar radiation, and ocean currents. These models are computationally intensive and require HPC to run efficiently. Climate researchers use HPC systems to explore different scenarios and predict the potential impacts of climate change on the environment and human society.

The Role of C# and .NET in HPC

Historically, high-performance computing has been dominated by low-level programming languages like C, C++, and Fortran, which offer fine-grained control over hardware resources and memory management. However, in recent years, C# and the .NET ecosystem have made significant strides in terms of performance, making them viable options for HPC applications. With the release of C# 10 and .NET 6, developers now have access to a modern, high-level programming language that offers both ease of use and the performance needed for HPC tasks.

1. Performance Improvements in .NET 6

One of the key reasons for the increasing popularity of C# and .NET in HPC is the performance improvements introduced in .NET 6. Microsoft has made significant optimizations to the .NET runtime, including:

- **Faster Memory Management**: .NET 6 includes improvements to the garbage collector (GC), which is responsible for managing memory in C# applications. These improvements reduce the overhead associated with memory allocation and deallocation, resulting in faster performance for memory-intensive applications.
- **Improved Just-In-Time (JIT) Compilation**: The JIT compiler in .NET 6 has been optimized to generate more efficient machine code, reducing the time required to execute C# programs. This is especially important for HPC applications, where performance is a critical concern.
- **Support for SIMD (Single Instruction, Multiple Data)**: .NET 6 includes support for SIMD, a technique that allows multiple data points to be processed simultaneously using a single instruction. SIMD is particularly useful in HPC applications that involve large-scale data processing, such as matrix computations and image processing.

2. Multi-Threading and Parallelism in C#

Another key feature of C# that makes it suitable for HPC is its robust support for multi-threading and parallelism. C# provides several tools for writing parallel code, including:

- **Task Parallel Library (TPL)**: The Task Parallel Library is a set of APIs that simplify the process of writing parallel code in C#. It allows developers to divide tasks into smaller sub-tasks that can be executed concurrently, improving performance in multi-core systems.
- **PLINQ (Parallel LINQ)**: PLINQ is an extension of LINQ (Language-Integrated Query) that allows developers to run queries in parallel. This is particularly useful in data-intensive applications, where parallelizing data processing tasks can significantly improve performance.

15

- **Async and Await**: C# 10 includes powerful asynchronous programming features that allow developers to write non-blocking code. This is essential for HPC applications that involve I/O-bound tasks, such as reading and writing large datasets from storage.

3. Cross-Platform Compatibility with .NET 6

One of the most significant advantages of using .NET 6 for HPC is its cross-platform compatibility. Unlike earlier versions of .NET, which were limited to Windows, .NET 6 is fully cross-platform, meaning that applications written in C# can run on Windows, Linux, and macOS. This is particularly important in HPC, where different parts of a distributed system may run on different operating systems. By using .NET 6, developers can write HPC applications that run on multiple platforms without needing to rewrite code for each environment.

In addition to running on different operating systems, .NET 6 also supports deployment in cloud environments, such as Microsoft Azure, AWS, and Google Cloud. This makes it easy to scale HPC applications in the cloud, taking advantage of the massive computational power offered by cloud providers.

4. Modern Language Features in C# 10

C# 10 includes several new language features that make it easier to write high-performance code. Some of these features include:

- **Record Structs**: Record structs are a new addition in C# 10 that allow developers to define immutable data types that are stored on the stack rather than the heap. This reduces the overhead associated with heap allocations, making record structs ideal for performance-critical applications.
- **Pattern Matching Enhancements**: C# 10 includes improvements to pattern matching, which allows developers to write more concise and efficient code. These enhancements make it easier to handle complex data processing tasks, such as parsing large datasets or processing complex data structures.

- **Global Usings and File-Scoped Namespaces**: These new features in C# 10 simplify code organization and reduce boilerplate, making it easier for developers to focus on writing performance-critical code without being bogged down by unnecessary syntax.

Conclusion

High-Performance Computing is transforming industries across the globe by enabling faster, more efficient processing of data and complex computations. With the advancements in C# 10 and .NET 6, developers now have a powerful, modern toolkit for building HPC applications that are both high-performing and easy to develop. By leveraging the features of C# and the performance optimizations in .NET 6, developers can create scalable, cross-platform HPC solutions that rival those built with more traditional low-level languages.

As the demand for HPC continues to grow, particularly in fields like artificial intelligence, data science, and financial modeling, the role of C# and .NET in this space will only become more prominent. The combination of developer productivity, modern language features, and cross-platform support makes C# and .NET 6 an attractive choice for organizations looking to harness the power of high-performance computing in their software development efforts.

Chapter 2: The Evolution of .NET and C# for Performance

Introduction

The landscape of software development is constantly evolving, and with each iteration, developers are met with new challenges and opportunities to optimize applications for better performance. In the past, high-performance computing (HPC) has been dominated by low-level programming languages such as C, C++, and Fortran, largely due to their ability to offer fine-grained control over system resources. However, with the introduction of .NET 6 and C# 10, Microsoft has taken significant strides to bring modern performance optimizations to a high-level language and its ecosystem.

This chapter explores the evolution of .NET and C# for performance, focusing on the key advancements introduced in .NET 6 and C# 10 that make these technologies more viable for high-performance computing tasks. We will compare previous versions of .NET with .NET 6 to demonstrate how far the platform has come and how it now competes with traditional HPC solutions.

Overview of .NET 6's Improvements for Performance

With .NET 6, Microsoft has delivered a unified platform that brings together the various implementations of .NET (such as .NET Core, Xamarin, and Mono) under a single framework. This not only simplifies development but also introduces several performance enhancements designed to make applications faster, more efficient, and more scalable. The following sections will cover some of the key improvements in .NET 6 that directly impact performance.

1. Just-In-Time (JIT) Compiler Improvements

One of the most significant performance improvements in .NET 6 comes from the optimizations made to the Just-In-Time (JIT) compiler. The JIT compiler is responsible for converting intermediate language (IL) code into native machine code at runtime, which is then executed by the operating system.

In previous versions of .NET, the JIT compiler was often a bottleneck, particularly in applications that required frequent recompilation of code. However, in .NET 6, Microsoft has made several enhancements to the JIT compiler that improve the speed and efficiency of this process.

- **Tiered Compilation**: Introduced in earlier versions of .NET Core but significantly improved in .NET 6, tiered compilation allows the runtime to initially compile methods using a fast, low-optimization strategy and then recompile them with higher optimization levels if they are executed frequently. This reduces startup time while still ensuring that hot paths (code executed frequently) are optimized for performance. Tiered compilation can result in significant performance gains for long-running applications, as frequently used code paths are optimized over time.

- **Improved Loop Optimization**: The JIT compiler in .NET 6 has been optimized to handle loops more efficiently. Loop unrolling and loop invariant code motion are techniques employed by the compiler to reduce the overhead of loop iterations and move computations that don't change across iterations outside of the loop. This optimization is especially beneficial for HPC applications where large loops are common.

- **Inlining Improvements**: Inlining is a process where the JIT compiler replaces a method call with the body of the method itself, reducing the overhead of the method call. .NET 6 includes smarter inlining heuristics, which help reduce function call overhead while ensuring that the benefits of inlining don't result in code bloat or increased memory usage.

2. Ahead-of-Time (AOT) Compilation

.NET 6 introduces native AOT compilation, which allows developers to precompile their applications into native code ahead of time, rather than relying on the JIT compiler at runtime. This brings several performance benefits:

- **Reduced Startup Time**: Since AOT eliminates the need for JIT compilation at runtime, applications start faster, making AOT particularly beneficial for scenarios where startup time is critical, such as command-line tools or cloud functions.
- **Smaller Memory Footprint**: AOT compilation produces smaller binaries compared to JIT-compiled applications because there is no need to store IL code and JIT-generated machine code in memory simultaneously.
- **Deterministic Performance**: AOT provides more consistent performance, as there are no JIT-related pauses during runtime. This is especially important in real-time or performance-sensitive applications, where unpredictable pauses for JIT compilation can affect performance negatively.

AOT is particularly useful in HPC environments where deterministic performance and reduced memory usage are critical.

3. Garbage Collection (GC) Enhancements

Garbage collection (GC) is a key feature of managed languages like C#, but it has historically been a source of performance issues in high-throughput applications. In .NET 6, Microsoft has introduced several improvements to the GC to minimize its impact on application performance.

- **Concurrent Garbage Collection**: In previous versions of .NET, GC pauses could cause noticeable performance degradation in applications, especially those handling large data sets. In .NET 6, the GC operates concurrently with application code, reducing the duration and frequency of pauses.
- **Large Object Heap (LOH) Improvements**: The Large Object Heap, which stores objects larger than 85,000 bytes, can be a source of performance bottlenecks in memory-intensive applications. .NET 6 includes optimizations that reduce fragmentation in the LOH and improve allocation performance for large objects.
- **Pinned Object Heap (POH)**: .NET 6 introduces a new heap type, the Pinned Object Heap, designed to manage objects that are pinned in memory (i.e., objects whose memory location cannot be moved by the GC). This reduces the negative impact that pinned objects have on the efficiency of the GC and improves overall memory management performance.

4. SIMD and Hardware Intrinsics Support

Single Instruction, Multiple Data (SIMD) is a parallel computing technique that allows the same operation to be performed on multiple data points simultaneously. SIMD is particularly useful for HPC applications that involve large-scale data processing, such as matrix computations, image processing, and scientific simulations.

In .NET 6, SIMD support has been expanded, allowing developers to take advantage of modern CPU architectures that support SIMD instructions. The Vector<T> type in .NET 6 enables developers to write SIMD-enabled code that can process multiple data points in parallel, resulting in significant performance improvements for certain types of calculations.

In addition to SIMD, .NET 6 also provides direct support for hardware intrinsics, which allow developers to use CPU-specific instructions (such as those found in Intel's AVX or ARM's NEON instruction sets) to optimize performance further. This low-level access to hardware features makes it possible to write highly optimized code that takes full advantage of modern processors.

5. Enhanced Asynchronous Programming with Async Streams

Asynchronous programming has become a critical component of modern applications, especially those that deal with I/O-bound tasks such as reading from disk or network communication. .NET 6 introduces several enhancements to asynchronous programming, including improvements to async streams.

- **Improved Async/Await Performance**: The async/await model in C# has been optimized to reduce overhead, particularly in scenarios where large numbers of asynchronous operations are created and awaited.
- **IAsyncEnumerable<T>**: The introduction of IAsyncEnumerable<T> in previous versions of .NET made it easier to work with asynchronous streams of data. .NET 6 further improves the performance of async streams, making it possible to process large amounts of data asynchronously with minimal overhead.

For HPC applications that involve data streams (e.g., processing sensor data, logs, or real-time analytics), the improvements in asynchronous programming in .NET 6 provide a significant performance boost.

Key Features of C# 10 for HPC

C# 10 builds upon the foundation of earlier versions of the language by introducing new features that enhance both developer productivity and performance. While many of the changes in C# 10 focus on improving the developer experience, several features are particularly beneficial for HPC applications, where performance is a top priority.

1. Record Structs

One of the most significant additions in C# 10 is the introduction of **record**

structs. Record structs are a lightweight, immutable data type that is stored on the stack rather than the heap. This has several performance implications:

- **Reduced Garbage Collection Pressure**: Since record structs are value types stored on the stack, they do not contribute to heap allocations and, therefore, do not add to the workload of the garbage collector. This is especially important in performance-critical applications, where frequent heap allocations can lead to performance degradation due to garbage collection pauses.
- **Improved Cache Locality**: Stack-allocated types like record structs benefit from better cache locality, as they are more likely to remain in the CPU cache, reducing the need to access slower main memory. This results in faster access times and improved overall performance.

Record structs are particularly useful in HPC applications where large numbers of small, immutable data structures are processed, such as in numerical simulations or real-time data analytics.

2. Global Usings and File-Scoped Namespaces

While these features may seem more focused on improving code readability and reducing boilerplate, they also have performance benefits, particularly in large-scale applications.

- **Global Usings**: In C# 10, developers can define global using directives that apply to all files in the project. This reduces the amount of redundant code and simplifies code organization. While this does not directly improve runtime performance, it can lead to faster build times and reduced code maintenance overhead, which can indirectly contribute to better application performance in large-scale HPC projects.
- **File-Scoped Namespaces**: File-scoped namespaces allow developers to declare a namespace for an entire file without requiring additional indentation. This reduces clutter in the code and improves readability, which can lead to more maintainable and optimized code in performance-critical applications.

3. Pattern Matching Enhancements

Pattern matching, introduced in earlier versions of C#, has been further enhanced in C# 10. The improvements to pattern matching make it easier to write concise, readable code while also improving performance in certain scenarios.

- **Improved Switch Expressions**: Switch expressions in C# 10 are more efficient and can handle more complex patterns with minimal overhead. This makes them particularly useful in applications that involve processing large datasets or complex data structures.
- **Recursive Pattern Matching**: Recursive patterns allow developers to match on nested data structures more efficiently, reducing the need for complex conditional logic and improving both readability and performance.

Pattern matching is especially useful in data-intensive HPC applications where complex data structures need to be processed efficiently.

4. Lambda Improvements

C# 10 introduces several enhancements to lambdas, which are frequently used in LINQ queries, parallel processing, and asynchronous programming.

- **Natural Type for Lambdas**: In previous versions of C#, developers often needed to explicitly declare the delegate type of a lambda expression. In C# 10, lambdas can infer their types naturally, simplifying the syntax and making code more readable.
- **Lambda Improvements in Performance**: The JIT compiler in .NET 6 has been optimized to handle lambdas more efficiently, reducing the overhead associated with creating and invoking lambdas. This is particularly beneficial in HPC applications that make heavy use of functional programming constructs like LINQ and PLINQ.

Comparing Previous .NET Versions to .NET 6

To truly appreciate the performance improvements in .NET 6, it's essential to compare it to previous versions of the .NET platform. While each new version of .NET has introduced performance enhancements, .NET 6 represents a significant leap forward in terms of both runtime optimizations and language features.

1. .NET Framework vs. .NET Core vs. .NET 6

The .NET Framework, first released in the early 2000s, was the original implementation of the .NET platform. However, it was primarily designed for Windows-based applications, and over time, its performance limitations became more apparent, particularly in the context of modern, high-performance applications.

- **.NET Framework**: While suitable for many enterprise applications, the .NET Framework's reliance on the Windows operating system and its relatively heavy runtime made it less than ideal for performance-critical applications. The garbage collector, in particular, was a frequent source of performance issues, as it was not optimized for low-latency, high-throughput workloads.

- **.NET Core**: In 2016, Microsoft introduced .NET Core, a cross-platform, open-source implementation of the .NET platform. .NET Core brought several performance improvements over the .NET Framework, including a more efficient garbage collector, better JIT compilation, and support for modern hardware features like SIMD. However, .NET Core was still a separate implementation, leading to fragmentation in the .NET ecosystem.

- **.NET 6**: With .NET 6, Microsoft has unified the various implementations of .NET (including .NET Core, Xamarin, and Mono) under a single platform. This unification not only simplifies development but also brings the best performance features from each implementation into a single runtime. The performance improvements in .NET 6, particularly in areas like JIT compilation, garbage collection, and AOT compilation, make it the most performant version of .NET to date.

2. Performance Gains in .NET 6

Several key metrics demonstrate the performance gains achieved in .NET 6 compared to previous versions:

- **Startup Time**: Thanks to AOT compilation and tiered JIT compilation, .NET 6 applications start faster than those built with previous versions of .NET. This is particularly important for cloud-based applications and command-line tools, where fast startup times are critical.
- **Throughput**: The improvements to garbage collection, SIMD support, and JIT optimizations in .NET 6 result in higher throughput for performance-critical applications. Benchmarks show that .NET 6 can handle more requests per second than previous versions, making it ideal for web services, APIs, and HPC workloads.
- **Memory Usage**: The enhanced garbage collector and memory management features in .NET 6 reduce the memory footprint of applications, making them more efficient in memory-constrained environments. This is especially important for applications running in containers or on cloud infrastructure, where memory usage directly impacts cost.

Conclusion

The evolution of .NET and C# for performance has been a journey marked by significant improvements at each stage. From the early days of the .NET Framework to the cross-platform capabilities of .NET Core and the unified platform of .NET 6, Microsoft has consistently worked to optimize the runtime and language for modern, high-performance applications.

With the introduction of .NET 6 and C# 10, developers now have access to a platform that combines ease of use with cutting-edge performance optimizations. Whether through the enhanced JIT compiler, improved garbage collection, support for SIMD, or the new features in C# 10, developers can build high-performance computing applications that rival those written in low-level languages like C or C++.

Chapter 3: Memory Management and Optimization in .NET 6

Effective memory management is a critical aspect of high-performance computing (HPC), as it directly influences application speed, resource consumption, and scalability. With the release of .NET 6, Microsoft introduced several enhancements to memory management that empower developers to write efficient, optimized applications. This chapter will delve into key aspects of memory management in .NET 6, focusing on the garbage collection (GC) system, the powerful Span<T> and Memory<T> types, and strategies for reducing heap allocations to minimize the performance impact of memory usage.

Understanding Garbage Collection in .NET

Garbage collection (GC) is a fundamental feature of .NET's memory management system. In a managed environment like .NET, developers do not need to explicitly allocate and deallocate memory, as the runtime automatically handles memory allocation and releases unused memory. This simplifies development and reduces memory-related bugs, but it also introduces potential performance challenges. Understanding how the GC system works and how it can be optimized is essential for building high-performance applications.

1. How Garbage Collection Works

The primary purpose of garbage collection is to reclaim memory that is no longer in use, freeing up resources for new objects. The GC system in .NET uses a **generational garbage collection model**, which organizes objects into different generations based on their lifespan.

- **Generation 0**: Newly allocated objects reside in Generation 0. These objects are typically short-lived, such as local variables and temporary data structures. The GC frequently collects Generation 0, as these objects tend to be discarded quickly.
- **Generation 1**: If an object survives a Generation 0 collection, it is promoted to Generation 1. Generation 1 serves as an intermediary step, containing objects with medium lifespans. These objects may survive a few garbage collection cycles but are still considered candidates for future collection.
- **Generation 2**: Objects that survive multiple collections are promoted to Generation 2, which contains long-lived objects. These objects, such as application state and static data, are less likely to be collected. Generation 2 collections occur less frequently than Generation 0 or 1 collections, as the cost of collecting Generation 2 is higher due to the increased volume of data.

The .NET GC operates in **two main modes**: **Workstation** and **Server** modes. Workstation mode is optimized for desktop applications, prioritizing low-latency garbage collection to maintain a smooth user experience. Server mode, on the other hand, is designed for high-throughput, multi-threaded applications such as web servers or HPC applications, where maximizing throughput is more important than minimizing pauses.

Phases of Garbage Collection

Garbage collection in .NET follows a structured approach, which can be broken down into several phases:

- **Mark Phase**: In the first phase, the garbage collector scans all active

29

(reachable) objects, starting from the root references (such as global variables, static fields, and active method stack frames). During this process, the collector marks all objects that are still in use.

- **Sweep Phase**: After marking the reachable objects, the garbage collector traverses through the heap to identify unreferenced (unreachable) objects. These objects are considered garbage and are subsequently marked for deallocation.

- **Compaction Phase**: To avoid fragmentation, the GC compacts the heap by moving all surviving objects into a contiguous memory block. This makes future allocations more efficient, as memory can be allocated in a contiguous chunk rather than searching for free space in a fragmented heap.

Each of these phases has performance implications. Frequent garbage collection cycles can introduce **GC pauses**, during which the application may experience brief delays. These pauses, though short, can become a bottleneck in memory-intensive applications if not properly managed.

2. Optimizing Garbage Collection for Performance

Efficient garbage collection is crucial for memory management, especially in high-performance environments. Here are several techniques and strategies for optimizing the garbage collection process in .NET 6:

a. Reducing Object Allocations

One of the most effective ways to minimize the impact of garbage collection is to reduce the number of objects allocated on the heap. The fewer objects the GC has to track, the less work it needs to do during a collection cycle. Developers can reduce allocations by:

- **Reusing Objects**: Instead of creating new objects each time a method is called, consider reusing existing objects. Object pooling is a common technique in which frequently used objects are stored in a pool and reused, reducing the need for new allocations.

- **Minimizing Temporary Allocations**: Temporary objects, such as those created within loops or frequently called methods, can quickly increase the number of objects in Generation 0. Using value types (stored on the stack) or optimizing the logic to reduce the creation of temporary objects can help mitigate this issue.

- **Avoiding Boxing/Unboxing**: Boxing occurs when a value type (such as an integer or struct) is converted into a reference type (an object). This process allocates memory on the heap, which can lead to additional GC overhead. Avoid unnecessary boxing and unboxing operations by using generics and value types where appropriate.

b. Tuning Garbage Collection Settings

In .NET 6, developers can adjust the behavior of the garbage collector to suit the specific needs of their applications. Key settings include:

- **Server vs. Workstation Mode**: As mentioned earlier, Workstation mode is suitable for low-latency applications, while Server mode is optimized for high-throughput applications. HPC applications typically benefit from Server mode, as it allows for more efficient garbage collection in multi-threaded environments.
- **Concurrent Garbage Collection**: Concurrent GC allows the garbage collector to run in the background while the application continues executing, reducing the impact of GC pauses. This feature is enabled by default in Workstation mode and can be enabled in Server mode for applications that require low-latency garbage collection.
- **Pinned Object Heap (POH)**: Introduced in .NET 5 and improved in .NET 6, the Pinned Object Heap is used to store objects that are pinned in memory (i.e., objects that the GC cannot move). Pinning objects in memory can lead to fragmentation, so .NET 6 introduces a separate heap for pinned objects to mitigate this issue.

c. Optimizing Large Object Heap (LOH) Usage

The **Large Object Heap (LOH)** stores objects larger than 85,000 bytes, such as large arrays or buffers. LOH collections can be expensive due to the size of the objects involved, so optimizing LOH usage is essential for high-performance applications.

- **Avoid Frequent LOH Allocations**: Avoiding frequent allocations of large objects reduces the need for LOH collections. Developers can break large objects into smaller chunks or use pooling techniques to reuse large objects instead of frequently allocating new ones.
- **Manual LOH Compaction**: While the garbage collector in .NET automatically compacts the small object heap, it does not automatically compact the LOH. In .NET 6, developers can trigger LOH compaction manually by using the GCSettings.LargeObjectHeapCompactionMode property. This is useful when fragmentation in the LOH becomes a performance issue.

Working with Span<T> and Memory<T>

In .NET 6, Span<T> and Memory<T> are two powerful types that provide low-level memory access and help developers avoid unnecessary heap allocations. These types are designed for performance-critical scenarios where efficient memory management is essential, making them highly relevant for HPC applications.

1. Understanding Span<T>

Span<T> is a **stack-allocated** type that represents a contiguous region of memory. Unlike traditional arrays or collections, Span<T> does not require heap allocation, making it highly efficient for working with slices of data. Key features of Span<T> include:

- **Stack Allocation**: Because Span<T> is stack-allocated, it does not require garbage collection, reducing the overall memory pressure on the system. This is particularly useful in performance-critical applications where frequent heap allocations could lead to GC overhead.
- **Safe Memory Access**: While Span<T> provides low-level access to memory, it still maintains the safety guarantees of C#. Developers cannot access out-of-bounds memory or create buffer overflows when

using Span<T>, making it a safer alternative to unsafe memory access techniques.

- **Slicing**: One of the most powerful features of Span<T> is its ability to create **slices** of data without copying the underlying memory. This allows developers to work with portions of an array or buffer without the overhead of creating new arrays. For example, developers can create a slice of an array that represents a subset of the data and pass it to methods without allocating new memory.

2. Understanding Memory<T>

While Span<T> is limited to stack-allocated memory, Memory<T> is a **heap-allocated** type that offers similar functionality but can be used in situations where the data is stored on the heap. Memory<T> is particularly useful when working with asynchronous or long-lived data structures that need to be passed around without allocating new memory.

- **Asynchronous Programming Support**: Unlike Span<T>, which cannot be used in asynchronous methods, Memory<T> can be used in situations where data needs to be passed across asynchronous method boundaries. This makes Memory<T> ideal for scenarios where data must be processed asynchronously, such as reading from a file or a network stream.
- **Interoperability with Span<T>**: Memory<T> can be easily converted into Span<T> using the Span property, allowing developers to use Span<T>'s efficient memory access features when working with heap-allocated data.

3. Using Span<T> and Memory<T> for High-Performance Memory Management

The combination of Span<T> and Memory<T> allows developers to write highly efficient memory management code without sacrificing safety or readability. Here are some common use cases for these types in high-performance applications:

a. Working with Arrays and Buffers

Span<T> can be used to create slices of arrays and buffers, allowing developers to work with subsets of data without allocating new memory. For example, if a method needs to process a portion of an array, Span<T> can be used to pass only the relevant data without creating a copy.

```csharp
Copy code
// Original array
int[] data = new int[] { 1, 2, 3, 4, 5, 6 };

// Create a Span that represents the first three elements
Span<int> span = data.AsSpan(0, 3);

// Process the Span
ProcessSpan(span);

void ProcessSpan(Span<int> data)
{
    // Perform operations on the span
}
```

This approach reduces memory allocations and improves performance by avoiding unnecessary copying of data.

b. Reducing Heap Allocations in String Manipulation

Span<T> is particularly useful in string manipulation tasks, where temporary strings are often created and discarded. Using Span<T>, developers can work directly with slices of strings without allocating new string objects, reducing the need for garbage collection.

```csharp
Copy code
string input = "Hello, World!";

// Create a span that represents the first five characters
ReadOnlySpan<char> span = input.AsSpan(0, 5);
```

```
// Use the span without allocating a new string
Console.WriteLine(span.ToString());  // Output: Hello
```

c. Optimizing I/O Operations

Memory<T> can be used to optimize I/O operations by reducing memory allocations in scenarios where large amounts of data are read from or written to files, streams, or network sockets.

For example, when reading from a file, developers can use Memory<T> to create a buffer that is passed across multiple asynchronous methods without allocating new buffers at each step.

```csharp
Copy code
async Task ProcessFileAsync(string filePath)
{
    byte[] buffer = new byte[1024]; // Buffer allocated once
    Memory<byte> memory = buffer.AsMemory();

    using FileStream fs = new FileStream(filePath, FileMode.Open,
    FileAccess.Read);

    while (true)
    {
        int bytesRead = await fs.ReadAsync(memory);
        if (bytesRead == 0) break;

        // Process the data in the buffer
        ProcessBuffer(memory.Span.Slice(0, bytesRead));
    }
}

void ProcessBuffer(Span<byte> data)
{
    // Perform operations on the data
}
```

This approach reduces the number of allocations and improves performance in I/O-bound applications.

Reducing Heap Allocations and Optimizing Memory Usage

Reducing heap allocations is one of the most effective ways to optimize memory usage in .NET applications. By minimizing the number of objects allocated on the heap, developers can reduce the workload of the garbage collector, leading to fewer GC pauses and better overall performance.

1. Object Pooling

Object pooling is a common technique for reducing heap allocations in performance-critical applications. Instead of creating new objects every time they are needed, a pool of reusable objects is maintained. When an object is no longer in use, it is returned to the pool rather than being garbage collected.

- **Benefits of Object Pooling**: Object pooling reduces the number of allocations and deallocations, which in turn reduces the frequency of garbage collection. This is especially useful for applications that create large numbers of short-lived objects, such as network servers or high-throughput data processors.

- **Implementing Object Pools**: .NET provides the ObjectPool<T> class as part of the Microsoft.Extensions.ObjectPool namespace, making it easy to implement object pooling in .NET applications.

```csharp
Copy code
ObjectPool<StringBuilder> pool = new
DefaultObjectPool<StringBuilder>(new
StringBuilderPooledObjectPolicy());

StringBuilder sb = pool.Get();
sb.Append("Hello, World!");

// Return the object to the pool when done
```

```
pool.Return(sb);
```

In this example, a StringBuilder is pooled, reducing the need for repeated allocations and garbage collection.

2. Value Types vs. Reference Types

Value types (such as structs) are allocated on the stack, while reference types (such as classes) are allocated on the heap. By using value types where appropriate, developers can reduce heap allocations and improve memory access patterns.

- **Avoiding Boxing and Unboxing**: Boxing occurs when a value type is converted to a reference type, leading to heap allocation. Avoid boxing by using generic methods and strongly typed collections.

```csharp
Copy code
// Avoid this: boxing occurs when adding the integer to the
ArrayList
ArrayList list = new ArrayList();
list.Add(42);  // This causes boxing

// Use a generic List<T> instead
List<int> list = new List<int>();
list.Add(42);  // No boxing
```

- **Choosing Value Types for Performance**: Value types are ideal for small, immutable data structures that are frequently used in performance-critical code. However, developers should avoid using value types for large, mutable data structures, as passing them by value can result in inefficient copying.

3. Avoiding Excessive Allocation of Temporary Objects

Temporary objects, such as those created within loops or frequently called methods, can quickly increase memory pressure, leading to frequent garbage collections. Minimizing the creation of temporary objects is a key strategy for optimizing memory usage.

- **Inlining Methods**: Inlining small methods that create temporary objects can reduce memory allocations, as the compiler can optimize the code to eliminate unnecessary object creation.
- **Avoiding LINQ in Performance-Critical Code**: While LINQ is convenient, it often results in the creation of temporary enumerators and other objects. In performance-critical code, consider using loops and manual iteration instead of LINQ to reduce the overhead of temporary object creation.

Conclusion

Memory management is a critical aspect of high-performance computing in .NET 6. By understanding how the garbage collection system works and utilizing tools like Span<T> and Memory<T>, developers can reduce heap allocations, optimize memory usage, and minimize the impact of garbage collection on application performance. Object pooling, careful use of value types, and minimizing temporary object creation are all effective strategies for optimizing memory management in .NET 6 applications.

Chapter 4: Asynchronous Programming for Performance

I n today's software development landscape, building responsive and high-performance applications is essential, especially in high-performance computing (HPC) scenarios. Asynchronous programming plays a pivotal role in achieving this goal by enabling applications to perform multiple tasks concurrently without blocking the main execution thread. This chapter will explore asynchronous programming in C# 10, focusing on the async and await keywords, task-based asynchronous programming, and techniques for optimizing asynchronous code for high performance.

1. Async and Await in C# 10

1.1 Understanding Asynchronous Programming

Asynchronous programming allows developers to write code that can initiate long-running operations without blocking the execution thread. In traditional synchronous programming, a thread would wait for a time-consuming operation (like file I/O or network requests) to complete before proceeding to the next line of code. This can lead to unresponsive applications, especially in user interfaces, where a blocked thread can make an application feel slow or unresponsive.

With asynchronous programming, developers can use constructs like async and await to offload time-consuming operations to the background while allowing the main thread to continue executing other code. This results in a more responsive application and better resource utilization.

1.2 The Async and Await Keywords

C# 10 introduced improvements to the async and await keywords, which are integral to implementing asynchronous programming in .NET applications.

- **Async**: The async keyword is used to declare an asynchronous method. An async method can contain await expressions, enabling the method to asynchronously wait for the completion of an operation.
- **Await**: The await keyword is used before a task that represents a long-running operation. When the execution reaches an await, control returns to the caller until the awaited task completes. This means the calling thread can continue executing other code, improving responsiveness.

1.3 Basic Structure of Asynchronous Methods

Here's a simple example of an asynchronous method in C#:

```csharp
Copy code
public async Task<int> GetDataAsync()
{
    // Simulate a long-running operation (e.g., a network request)
    await Task.Delay(2000); // Asynchronously wait for 2 seconds
    return 42; // Return some data
}
```

In this example, GetDataAsync is an asynchronous method that simulates a delay of two seconds before returning the value 42. When called, this method will not block the calling thread; instead, it will allow other operations to continue while waiting for the delay to complete.

40

1.4 Handling Exceptions in Asynchronous Methods

Exception handling in asynchronous methods follows the same principles as synchronous methods, but developers must be aware that exceptions may not be thrown until the awaited task is completed.

```csharp
Copy code
public async Task<int> GetDataWithErrorAsync()
{
    try
    {
        await Task.Delay(2000);
        throw new InvalidOperationException("An error occurred.");
    }
    catch (Exception ex)
    {
        Console.WriteLine($"Error: {ex.Message}");
        return -1; // Handle the error appropriately
    }
}
```

In this example, the exception is caught within the async method, allowing developers to handle errors gracefully without crashing the application.

2. Task-Based Asynchronous Programming

2.1 The Task Class

At the heart of asynchronous programming in C# is the Task class, which represents an asynchronous operation. The Task class provides methods and properties to manage the execution of asynchronous code.

- **Creating Tasks**: Developers can create tasks using Task.Run or by directly instantiating a Task.

```
csharp
Copy code
Task<int> task = Task.Run(() =>
{
    // Perform some computation
    return 42;
});
```

- **Task Completion**: The Task class has properties like IsCompleted, IsFaulted, and IsCanceled, which provide information about the task's state. Developers can check these properties to manage the execution flow based on the task's outcome.

2.2 Task vs. ValueTask

While Task is the most commonly used type for representing asynchronous operations, C# also introduces ValueTask for performance-critical scenarios.

- **Task**: Represents an asynchronous operation that may complete asynchronously. When a Task is awaited, it may involve heap allocation and garbage collection.
- **ValueTask**: A lightweight alternative to Task designed to avoid allocations in scenarios where the result may be available synchronously. ValueTask can be beneficial in high-performance scenarios, especially for methods that frequently return results without needing to perform an asynchronous operation.

Here's an example:

```
csharp
Copy code
```

```
public ValueTask<int> GetValueTaskAsync()
{
    if (/* condition to return synchronously */)
    {
        return new ValueTask<int>(42); // Return immediately
    }
    else
    {
        return new ValueTask<int>(Task.Delay(2000).ContinueWith(t
        => 42)); // Return asynchronously
    }
}
```

2.3 Chaining Asynchronous Tasks

Developers can chain asynchronous tasks to create more complex workflows.
When one task depends on the result of another, await can be used in sequence
to ensure proper execution order.

```csharp
Copy code
public async Task<int> ProcessDataAsync()
{
    int data = await GetDataAsync();
    // Process the data
    return data * 2; // Return processed data
}
```

In this example, ProcessDataAsync waits for GetDataAsync to complete
before processing the result.

2.4 Asynchronous Streams with IAsyncEnumerable

C# 8 introduced asynchronous streams, allowing developers to work with streams of data asynchronously. By using IAsyncEnumerable<T>, developers can iterate over asynchronous data sources without blocking the calling thread.

```csharp
Copy code
public async IAsyncEnumerable<int> GetNumbersAsync()
{
    for (int i = 0; i < 10; i++)
    {
        await Task.Delay(500); // Simulate an asynchronous
        operation
        yield return i; // Yield numbers asynchronously
    }
}
```

2.5 Consuming Asynchronous Streams

To consume an asynchronous stream, developers can use await foreach, which allows iteration over the results without blocking:

```csharp
Copy code
public async Task ConsumeNumbersAsync()
{
    await foreach (int number in GetNumbersAsync())
    {
        Console.WriteLine(number);
    }
}
```

Asynchronous streams are particularly useful when processing data that arrives over time, such as reading lines from a file or handling real-time updates from a network source.

3. Optimizing Asynchronous Code for High Performance

While asynchronous programming offers many advantages, poorly implemented asynchronous code can lead to performance issues. To ensure high
performance in asynchronous applications, developers should consider the
following optimization strategies:

3.1 Avoiding Async Overhead

While the async and await keywords simplify asynchronous programming,
they can introduce overhead if used improperly. Here are strategies to
minimize this overhead:

- **Use Async Methods Judiciously**: Not every method needs to be
  asynchronous. Use asynchronous programming for operations that are
  inherently I/O-bound (e.g., network requests, file I/O). Avoid marking
  methods as async if they only perform CPU-bound computations.
- **Minimize the Number of Await Calls**: Each await incurs a state
  machine overhead, which can lead to increased memory usage and
  performance degradation. Try to batch operations or minimize the
  number of await calls within critical paths.

3.2 Avoiding Blocking Calls

Blocking calls within asynchronous methods can negate the benefits of
asynchronous programming. Ensure that long-running operations are
properly awaited rather than blocking the thread:

- **Use Asynchronous APIs**: Opt for asynchronous versions of methods whenever possible. For example, use File.ReadAsync instead of
  File.ReadAllText, or HttpClient.GetAsync instead of WebClient.Dow

nloadString.

- **Avoid .Result and .Wait()**: Accessing the .Result property or calling .Wait() on tasks blocks the calling thread, defeating the purpose of asynchronous programming. Instead, always use await.

3.3 Optimizing Exception Handling

Exception handling in asynchronous code can impact performance if not done carefully. When exceptions occur in asynchronous methods, they are captured in the task and can lead to performance degradation if not managed properly.

- **Use Try-Catch Judiciously**: Wrap only the code that may throw exceptions within a try-catch block. Avoid wrapping the entire asynchronous method, as this can lead to unnecessary overhead.

```csharp
Copy code
public async Task<int> SafeGetDataAsync()
{
    try
    {
        return await GetDataAsync();
    }
    catch (Exception ex)
    {
        // Handle specific exceptions
        return -1; // Return a default value or log the error
    }
}
```

- **Consider Exception Aggregation**: If a method may throw multiple exceptions, consider aggregating them into a single exception to reduce overhead.

3.4 Efficient Use of Cancellation Tokens

In long-running asynchronous operations, it's important to provide a way to cancel tasks to free up resources and improve responsiveness. C# provides the CancellationToken struct to handle cancellations effectively.

- **Accept Cancellation Tokens**: Modify methods to accept a CancellationToken parameter, allowing callers to request cancellation of the operation.

```csharp
Copy code
public async Task<int>
GetDataWithCancellationAsync(CancellationToken cancellationToken)
{
    await Task.Delay(2000, cancellationToken); // Pass the token
    to async methods
    return 42;
}
```

- **Check for Cancellation**: Within long-running operations, regularly check if cancellation has been requested and exit early if necessary.

```csharp
Copy code
if (cancellationToken.IsCancellationRequested)
{
    return -1; // Return or throw an exception
}
```

3.5 Managing Context with ConfigureAwait

By default, when using await, the continuation of the asynchronous operation resumes on the original synchronization context. In UI applications, this is usually the UI thread, but in server applications, it can lead to performance bottlenecks.

- **Use ConfigureAwait(false)**: To avoid capturing the synchronization context and improve performance, use ConfigureAwait(false) on await calls in library code or non-UI scenarios.

```csharp
Copy code
await GetDataAsync().ConfigureAwait(false);
```

Using ConfigureAwait(false) reduces the overhead of marshaling back to the original context, especially in high-throughput server applications.

3.6 Profiling and Benchmarking Asynchronous Code

To ensure that asynchronous code performs optimally, developers should regularly profile and benchmark their applications.

- **Use Profiling Tools**: Tools like Visual Studio Profiler, JetBrains dotTrace, or PerfView can help identify bottlenecks in asynchronous code, allowing developers to make data-driven optimizations.
- **Benchmarking Libraries**: Libraries such as BenchmarkDotNet can be used to measure the performance of asynchronous methods, helping developers understand the impact of various optimizations.

3.7 Best Practices for Asynchronous Programming

In addition to the optimization strategies discussed, here are some best practices for writing efficient asynchronous code in C#:

- **Favor Task-Based Asynchronous Methods**: When designing APIs, prefer using Task or ValueTask to represent asynchronous operations. This allows consumers to use await seamlessly.
- **Avoid Fire-and-Forget Tasks**: Fire-and-forget tasks can lead to unhandled exceptions and resource leaks. If a task is started asynchronously, ensure that it is awaited or handled properly.
- **Utilize Asynchronous Patterns**: Familiarize yourself with asynchronous programming patterns, such as producer-consumer or event-driven models, to make the most of asynchronous programming.
- **Document Asynchronous Behavior**: Clearly document the asynchronous nature of methods in your APIs to ensure that consumers understand how to use them correctly.

Conclusion

Asynchronous programming is a powerful tool for building responsive, high-performance applications in C#. By leveraging the async and await keywords, developers can write clean, maintainable code that executes efficiently. With enhancements in C# 10 and .NET 6, asynchronous programming becomes even more accessible and efficient, particularly in high-performance computing scenarios.

Chapter 5: Multithreading and Parallel Programming

A s the demand for high-performance applications increases, multithreading and parallel programming have emerged as essential techniques in software development. They allow applications to perform multiple tasks concurrently, improving resource utilization and performance. In this chapter, we will explore the concepts of multithreading and parallel programming in the context of C# and .NET 6. We will cover the fundamentals of creating and managing threads, the Task Parallel Library (TPL), Parallel LINQ (PLINQ), and best practices for writing efficient multithreaded applications.

1. Understanding Multithreading

1.1 What is Multithreading?

Multithreading is a programming paradigm that allows multiple threads to execute concurrently within a single process. A thread is the smallest unit of processing that can be scheduled by the operating system. By utilizing multiple threads, developers can perform various operations simultaneously, improving application responsiveness and throughput.

Multithreading is particularly useful in scenarios where tasks can run independently of one another. For example, in a graphical user interface (GUI) application, the UI thread can remain responsive to user input while background threads handle time-consuming tasks, such as data loading or calculations.

1.2 Benefits of Multithreading

The benefits of multithreading include:

- **Improved Responsiveness**: Applications that utilize multithreading can remain responsive to user interactions, even when performing lengthy operations. This enhances the user experience by preventing the application from freezing or becoming unresponsive.
- **Better Resource Utilization**: Modern processors are typically multi-core, meaning they can execute multiple threads simultaneously. By leveraging multithreading, applications can fully utilize the available CPU resources, leading to better performance.
- **Concurrent Processing**: Multithreading allows developers to perform multiple tasks concurrently, such as making network requests, performing calculations, or processing data. This can significantly reduce the overall execution time for applications that need to perform multiple independent operations.

1.3 Challenges of Multithreading

While multithreading offers numerous benefits, it also presents challenges that developers must address:

- **Complexity**: Writing multithreaded code can be more complex than writing single-threaded code. Developers must manage thread lifecycle, synchronization, and communication between threads, increasing the potential for errors and bugs.
- **Race Conditions**: When multiple threads access shared resources

51

simultaneously, race conditions can occur. This leads to unpredictable behavior, as the outcome depends on the timing of thread execution.

- **Deadlocks**: Deadlocks occur when two or more threads are waiting for each other to release resources, leading to a situation where none of the threads can proceed. Proper synchronization techniques must be employed to prevent deadlocks.

2. Creating and Managing Threads in C#

2.1 The Thread Class

In C#, the Thread class provides a way to create and manage threads. To create a new thread, developers instantiate a Thread object and pass a delegate (method) that represents the work to be performed.

```csharp
Copy code
using System;
using System.Threading;

class Program
{
    static void Main()
    {
        Thread thread = new Thread(WorkMethod);
        thread.Start(); // Start the thread
        thread.Join(); // Wait for the thread to finish
        Console.WriteLine("Thread has completed.");
    }

    static void WorkMethod()
    {
        Console.WriteLine("Working in a separate thread...");
        // Simulate some work
        Thread.Sleep(2000);
    }
```

```
}
```

In this example, a new thread is created to execute the WorkMethod. The Start method initiates the thread, while Join is called to wait for the thread to complete before proceeding.

2.2 Thread States and Lifecycle

Threads in C# can be in different states throughout their lifecycle:

- **Unstarted**: The thread is created but has not yet started executing.
- **Running**: The thread is actively executing its assigned method.
- **Blocked**: The thread is waiting for a resource or event, preventing it from executing.
- **Stopped**: The thread has completed execution and is no longer running.

Understanding these states is essential for managing threads effectively and avoiding common pitfalls like deadlocks and race conditions.

2.3 Thread Synchronization

To manage access to shared resources among multiple threads, synchronization techniques must be employed. Common synchronization mechanisms in C# include:

- **Lock Statements**: The lock statement provides a simple way to ensure that only one thread can access a critical section of code at a time. It prevents race conditions by blocking other threads from entering the locked section until the lock is released.

```csharp
Copy code
private static readonly object _lock = new object();

public void SafeMethod()
{
    lock (_lock)
    {
        // Critical section: only one thread can enter here at a
        time
        // Perform operations on shared resources
    }
}
```

- **Monitor Class**: The Monitor class provides more advanced synchronization capabilities, allowing developers to manually control locks, wait for conditions, and signal other threads.
- **Mutex**: A Mutex is a synchronization primitive that can be used to manage access to resources across multiple processes. Unlike a lock, which is confined to a single process, a Mutex can synchronize threads in different processes.
- **Semaphore**: A Semaphore allows a specified number of threads to access a resource concurrently. This is useful for managing limited resources, such as database connections or file handles.

2.4 Thread Pooling

Creating and managing individual threads can be resource-intensive. The .NET framework provides a built-in thread pool that efficiently manages a pool of worker threads. By using the thread pool, developers can avoid the overhead of thread creation and destruction.

- **ThreadPool Class**: The ThreadPool class allows developers to queue work items to be executed by worker threads in the pool.

```csharp
Copy code
ThreadPool.QueueUserWorkItem(WorkMethod);

static void WorkMethod(object state)
{
    Console.WriteLine("Working in a thread pool thread...");
}
```

Using the thread pool is particularly beneficial in scenarios where many short-lived tasks need to be executed concurrently, as it reduces the overhead of creating and destroying threads.

3. Task-Based Asynchronous Programming

3.1 Introduction to Task-Based Asynchronous Programming

Task-based asynchronous programming provides a more efficient and manageable way to work with asynchronous operations in C#. The Task class represents an asynchronous operation and is part of the Task Parallel Library (TPL), which simplifies the process of writing concurrent code.

3.2 Creating and Running Tasks

To create and run tasks, developers can use the Task.Run method, which schedules a task to run asynchronously on a thread pool thread:

```csharp
Copy code
Task task = Task.Run(() =>
{
    // Perform some work
    Thread.Sleep(2000);
```

```
    Console.WriteLine("Task completed.");
});
```

In this example, the task performs a long-running operation without blocking the calling thread.

3.3 Chaining Tasks with Continuations

Tasks can be chained together using continuations, which allow developers to specify what should happen when a task completes. This can be done using the ContinueWith method.

```csharp
Copy code
Task task = Task.Run(() =>
{
    // Perform work
    return 42; // Return a result
}).ContinueWith(t =>
{
    // This runs after the previous task completes
    Console.WriteLine($"Result: {t.Result}");
});
```

Chaining tasks simplifies the flow of asynchronous code and makes it easier to handle results or errors from previous tasks.

3.4 Exception Handling with Tasks

Exception handling in task-based asynchronous programming is crucial for managing errors that occur during asynchronous operations. If a task throws an exception, the exception is captured and can be retrieved using the Exception property of the completed task.

```csharp
Copy code
Task task = Task.Run(() =>
{
    throw new InvalidOperationException("An error occurred.");
});

try
{
    task.Wait(); // Wait for the task to complete
}
catch (AggregateException ex)
{
    // Handle exceptions thrown by the task
    foreach (var innerEx in ex.InnerExceptions)
    {
        Console.WriteLine(innerEx.Message);
    }
}
```

In this example, the task throws an exception, which is caught when waiting for the task to complete.

3.5 Async/Await with Tasks

The async and await keywords work seamlessly with tasks, providing a clean syntax for asynchronous programming. When a method is marked as async, it can use await to pause execution until the awaited task completes:

```csharp
Copy code
public async Task<int> GetDataAsync()
{
    await Task.Delay(2000); // Simulate a delay
    return 42; // Return a result
}
```

Using async and await simplifies the code and improves readability, making it easier to understand the flow of asynchronous operations.

3.6 Task Cancellation

Task cancellation is an essential aspect of managing long-running operations. The CancellationToken structure allows developers to signal tasks to cancel their work.

```csharp
Copy code
public async Task<int>
GetDataWithCancellationAsync(CancellationToken cancellationToken)
{
    await Task.Delay(5000, cancellationToken); // Support
    cancellation
    return 42; // Return a result
}
```

In this example, the await call will throw an OperationCanceledException if the cancellation token is triggered while the task is waiting.

3.7 Combining Tasks with Task.WhenAll and Task.WhenAny

In scenarios where multiple tasks need to be executed concurrently, developers can use Task.WhenAll and Task.WhenAny to manage their execution.

- **Task.WhenAll:** This method takes multiple tasks and returns a single task that completes when all of the specified tasks have completed.

```csharp
Copy code
Task<int> task1 = GetDataAsync();
Task<int> task2 = GetDataAsync();
```

```
int[] results = await Task.WhenAll(task1, task2);
```

- **Task.WhenAny**: This method returns a task that completes when any of the specified tasks completes. This is useful when you want to take action based on the first task to finish.

```csharp
Copy code
Task<int> task1 = GetDataAsync();
Task<int> task2 = GetDataAsync();

Task<int> completedTask = await Task.WhenAny(task1, task2);
int result = await completedTask; // Get the result of the
completed task
```

3.8 Best Practices for Task-Based Asynchronous Programming

To write efficient and maintainable asynchronous code, developers should adhere to several best practices:

- **Prefer Task-Based APIs**: Use asynchronous APIs that return Task or ValueTask whenever possible, as they provide a natural way to work with asynchronous operations.
- **Use Cancellation Tokens**: Always support cancellation in long-running tasks to improve responsiveness and resource management.
- **Avoid Blocking Calls**: Do not use .Result or .Wait() on tasks, as these will block the calling thread and defeat the purpose of asynchronous programming.
- **Consider Task Creation Overhead**: For short-lived operations, consider using ValueTask to reduce the overhead of creating tasks and

minimize garbage collection pressure.

4. Parallel Programming with TPL

4.1 Introduction to Parallel Programming

Parallel programming is a programming paradigm that allows developers to divide a problem into smaller sub-problems that can be solved concurrently. In the context of .NET, the Task Parallel Library (TPL) provides a set of APIs for writing parallel code easily and efficiently.

4.2 Using Parallel.For and Parallel.ForEach

The Parallel.For and Parallel.ForEach methods enable developers to run loops in parallel, distributing the workload across multiple threads automatically.

- **Parallel.For**: This method allows developers to execute a loop in parallel, improving performance for CPU-bound operations.

```csharp
Copy code
Parallel.For(0, 1000, i =>
{
    // Perform operations in parallel
    Console.WriteLine($"Processing {i} on thread
    {Thread.CurrentThread.ManagedThreadId}");
});
```

- **Parallel.ForEach**: This method works similarly but operates on collections, allowing developers to process each element in parallel.

```csharp
Copy code
var numbers = Enumerable.Range(0, 1000);
Parallel.ForEach(numbers, number =>
{
    Console.WriteLine($"Processing {number} on thread
    {Thread.CurrentThread.ManagedThreadId}");
});
```

Both Parallel.For and Parallel.ForEach automatically manage the partitioning of work and thread allocation, making it easy to take advantage of multi-core processors.

4.3 Managing Exceptions in Parallel Loops

When using parallel loops, exceptions can occur in multiple iterations. To handle exceptions properly, developers should use the ParallelLoopResult structure.

```csharp
Copy code
try
{
    Parallel.For(0, 1000, i =>
    {
        if (i == 500) throw new InvalidOperationException("An
        error occurred.");
    });
}
catch (AggregateException ex)
{
    foreach (var innerEx in ex.InnerExceptions)
    {
        Console.WriteLine($"Error: {innerEx.Message}");
    }
}
```

4.4 Parallel LINQ (PLINQ)

Parallel LINQ (PLINQ) extends LINQ by enabling parallel processing of collections. By using PLINQ, developers can write queries that run concurrently, taking advantage of multiple cores.

```csharp
Copy code
var numbers = Enumerable.Range(1, 1000000);

// Perform a parallel LINQ query
var results = numbers.AsParallel()
                .Where(n => n % 2 == 0)
                .Select(n => n * n)
                .ToArray();
```

In this example, the query processes numbers in parallel, significantly improving performance for large collections.

4.5 Controlling PLINQ Execution

PLINQ provides several options for controlling parallel execution, including:

- **WithDegreeOfParallelism**: This option allows developers to specify the maximum degree of parallelism (the number of concurrent tasks).

```csharp
Copy code
var results = numbers.AsParallel()
                .WithDegreeOfParallelism(4) // Limit to 4
                concurrent tasks
                .Where(n => n % 2 == 0)
                .Select(n => n * n)
                .ToArray();
```

- **AsOrdered**: By default, PLINQ does not guarantee the order of results. The AsOrdered method can be used to maintain the order of elements.

```csharp
Copy code
var orderedResults = numbers.AsParallel()
                    .AsOrdered()
                    .Where(n => n % 2 == 0)
                    .ToArray();
```

4.6 Best Practices for Parallel Programming

To maximize the benefits of parallel programming in C#, developers should follow these best practices:

- **Identify Parallelizable Workloads**: Before using parallel programming, analyze the workload to determine if it can be effectively divided into independent tasks.
- **Limit Overhead**: Parallelizing small tasks can introduce overhead due to thread management. Ensure that tasks are sufficiently large to justify parallel execution.
- **Avoid Shared State**: Minimize shared state between parallel tasks to reduce the risk of race conditions and the need for synchronization.
- **Use Appropriate Data Structures**: When working with parallel programming, consider using thread-safe collections or data structures that support concurrent access.

5. Best Practices for Multithreading and Parallel Programming

5.1 Profiling and Benchmarking

To ensure that multithreaded and parallel applications perform optimally, developers should regularly profile and benchmark their code. This allows them to identify performance bottlenecks and make data-driven optimizations.

- **Use Profiling Tools**: Tools like Visual Studio Profiler, JetBrains dotTrace, or PerfView can help analyze thread usage, memory consumption, and CPU utilization.
- **Benchmarking Libraries**: Libraries such as BenchmarkDotNet can be used to measure the performance of multithreaded and parallel code, helping developers understand the impact of various optimizations.

5.2 Avoiding Deadlocks and Race Conditions

Deadlocks and race conditions are common pitfalls in multithreaded programming. To avoid these issues:

- **Use Lock Hierarchy**: When multiple locks are required, establish a consistent order in which locks are acquired to prevent circular dependencies.
- **Minimize Lock Scope**: Keep the scope of locks as narrow as possible to reduce contention among threads. Only lock the critical section of code that requires synchronization.
- **Use Higher-Level Concurrency Primitives**: Consider using higher-level constructs like ConcurrentQueue, ConcurrentBag, or BlockingCollection instead of manually managing locks.

5.3 Testing and Debugging Multithreaded Applications

Testing and debugging multithreaded applications can be challenging due to the inherent complexity and non-deterministic nature of thread execution. To effectively test and debug multithreaded code:

- **Use Unit Testing**: Write unit tests for individual components and ensure that they behave correctly in both single-threaded and multithreaded scenarios.
- **Logging and Tracing**: Incorporate logging and tracing in multithreaded applications to capture the flow of execution and help identify issues.
- **Debugging Tools**: Utilize debugging tools and techniques that support multithreaded applications, such as Visual Studio's threading window or specialized tools like Concurrency Visualizer.

5.4 Documentation and Code Readability

Maintainability is crucial in multithreaded and parallel programming. To enhance code readability and maintainability:

- **Comment Code**: Document the purpose of multithreaded code, synchronization mechanisms, and any potential pitfalls that developers should be aware of.
- **Use Descriptive Names**: Use clear and descriptive names for methods, classes, and variables to convey their purpose and improve code readability.

Conclusion

Multithreading and parallel programming are essential techniques for building high-performance applications in C#. By leveraging the power of the Task Parallel Library, PLINQ, and effective synchronization techniques, developers can create responsive, efficient applications that take full advantage of modern multi-core processors.

While multithreading and parallel programming offer numerous benefits, they also present challenges that require careful consideration and planning. By following best practices, conducting thorough testing, and profiling performance, developers can create robust applications that meet the demands of high-performance computing.

Chapter 6: Task-Based Asynchronous Programming with TPL

In the realm of high-performance computing (HPC) and modern application development, effective management of asynchronous operations is critical for creating responsive and scalable applications. The Task Parallel Library (TPL) in .NET provides a powerful framework for implementing task-based asynchronous programming, allowing developers to easily manage concurrent operations, streamline workflows, and optimize resource utilization. In this chapter, we will explore TPL in detail, covering its core concepts, features, and best practices for using it effectively in C#.

1. Introduction to the Task Parallel Library (TPL)

1.1 What is TPL?

The Task Parallel Library (TPL) is a set of public types and APIs in the .NET Framework that enable developers to write parallel and asynchronous code easily. Introduced in .NET Framework 4, TPL simplifies the process of creating and managing tasks, which represent asynchronous operations. TPL abstracts the complexities of thread management and provides a high-level API for working with parallelism and concurrency.

1.2 The Importance of TPL in Modern Applications

As applications increasingly rely on multi-core processors and asynchronous I/O operations, the need for efficient parallel programming becomes paramount. The TPL allows developers to leverage the full capabilities of modern hardware without getting bogged down in the low-level details of thread management. Key benefits of TPL include:

- **Simplified Development**: TPL provides a straightforward way to create, run, and manage tasks, reducing the amount of boilerplate code needed for asynchronous programming.
- **Improved Performance**: By allowing developers to write parallel code, TPL can significantly improve application performance, especially for CPU-bound operations.
- **Better Resource Management**: TPL manages the allocation and scheduling of threads efficiently, ensuring optimal resource utilization and minimizing overhead.

2. Core Concepts of TPL

2.1 Tasks and Task Types

At the heart of TPL are tasks, which represent asynchronous operations that can be executed concurrently. The Task class is the primary type used to create and manage tasks.

2.1.1 Creating Tasks

Tasks can be created using various methods, including Task.Run, Task.Fact ory.StartNew, or by instantiating a Task directly. Here's how to create a task using Task.Run:

```csharp
Copy code
```

```
Task task = Task.Run(() =>
{
    // Perform some work asynchronously
    Thread.Sleep(2000); // Simulate a delay
    Console.WriteLine("Task completed.");
});
```

2.1.2 Task Types

In addition to the standard Task type, TPL provides Task<T>, which represents an asynchronous operation that returns a result. This allows developers to work with return values easily.

```
csharp
Copy code
Task<int> taskWithResult = Task.Run(() =>
{
    Thread.Sleep(2000); // Simulate a delay
    return 42; // Return a result
});
```

2.2 Task States

Tasks have various states that indicate their progress and completion:

- **Created**: The task has been instantiated but has not yet started executing.
- **Running**: The task is currently executing.
- **Completed**: The task has finished executing, whether it completed successfully or failed.
- **Faulted**: The task encountered an exception during execution.
- **Canceled**: The task was canceled before it could complete.

Developers can check the state of a task using properties like IsCompleted, IsFaulted, and IsCanceled.

2.3 Chaining Tasks with Continuations

One of the powerful features of TPL is the ability to chain tasks using continuations. When a task completes, developers can specify another action to be executed as a continuation. This can be achieved using the ContinueWith method.

```csharp
Copy code
Task<int> task = Task.Run(() =>
{
    // Perform some work
    return 42;
}).ContinueWith(t =>
{
    // This runs after the previous task completes
    Console.WriteLine($"Result: {t.Result}");
});
```

This approach allows for clean, readable code that clearly outlines the flow of asynchronous operations.

2.4 Exception Handling with Tasks

Exception handling in TPL is straightforward but requires attention to detail. If a task throws an exception, the exception is captured and can be retrieved later.

```csharp
Copy code
Task task = Task.Run(() =>
{
    throw new InvalidOperationException("An error occurred.");
});
```

```
try
{
    task.Wait(); // Wait for the task to complete
}
catch (AggregateException ex)
{
    foreach (var innerEx in ex.InnerExceptions)
    {
        Console.WriteLine($"Error: {innerEx.Message}");
    }
}
```

In this example, the exception thrown by the task is caught when waiting for the task to complete.

3. Async/Await in TPL

3.1 Using Async and Await

The async and await keywords simplify asynchronous programming in C#. When a method is marked as async, it can contain await expressions, allowing it to pause execution until the awaited task completes.

```csharp
Copy code
public async Task<int> GetDataAsync()
{
    await Task.Delay(2000); // Simulate a delay
    return 42; // Return a result
}
```

In this example, the method GetDataAsync is asynchronous and pauses for 2 seconds before returning a value.

3.2 Benefits of Async/Await with TPL

The combination of async/await and TPL provides several advantages:

- **Improved Readability**: Asynchronous code using async and await is often more readable than traditional callback-based code, making it easier to understand and maintain.
- **Simplified Exception Handling**: Exception handling becomes more straightforward, as exceptions can be caught using standard try-catch blocks.
- **Enhanced Responsiveness**: By allowing the main thread to continue executing while awaiting long-running operations, applications remain responsive to user interactions.

3.3 Common Patterns with Async/Await

Developers often use async and await with common patterns, such as:

- **Sequential Operations**: Awaiting multiple asynchronous operations in sequence:

```csharp
Copy code
public async Task ProcessDataAsync()
{
    int data1 = await GetDataAsync();
    int data2 = await GetDataAsync();
    // Process the data
}
```

- **Concurrent Operations**: Running multiple asynchronous operations concurrently using Task.WhenAll:

```csharp
Copy code
public async Task ProcessMultipleDataAsync()
{
    Task<int> task1 = GetDataAsync();
    Task<int> task2 = GetDataAsync();

    int[] results = await Task.WhenAll(task1, task2);
    // Process results
}
```

3.4 Handling Cancellations in Async Methods

Cancellation is an essential feature of asynchronous programming, allowing developers to cancel long-running operations. The CancellationToken struct provides a mechanism for requesting cancellation.

```csharp
Copy code
public async Task<int>
GetDataWithCancellationAsync(CancellationToken cancellationToken)
{
    await Task.Delay(2000, cancellationToken); // Support
    cancellation
    return 42; // Return a result
}
```

In this example, if the cancellation token is triggered, the awaited task will throw an OperationCanceledException, allowing the application to handle cancellations gracefully.

4. Best Practices for Task-Based Asynchronous Programming

4.1 Avoid Blocking Calls

One of the fundamental principles of asynchronous programming is to avoid blocking calls, as they can negate the benefits of async and await. Avoid using .Result or .Wait() on tasks, as these will block the calling thread.

4.2 Use Asynchronous APIs

When designing APIs, prefer using asynchronous versions of methods that return Task or ValueTask. This allows consumers to work with the asynchronous nature of the API seamlessly.

4.3 Implement Cancellation Support

Always support cancellation in long-running asynchronous operations. This improves responsiveness and allows users to stop operations when they are no longer needed.

4.4 Minimize State Capture

By default, await captures the current synchronization context, which can lead to unnecessary context switching and performance overhead. Use ConfigureAwait(false) to avoid capturing the context when it's not needed.

```csharp
Copy code
await GetDataAsync().ConfigureAwait(false);
```

4.5 Profile and Benchmark

Regularly profile and benchmark asynchronous code to identify performance bottlenecks. Use profiling tools and benchmarking libraries to measure the impact of optimizations and ensure optimal performance.

5. Parallel Programming with TPL

5.1 Introduction to Parallel Programming

Parallel programming is a programming paradigm that divides a problem into smaller sub-problems that can be solved concurrently. The Task Parallel Library (TPL) in .NET provides a set of APIs for writing parallel code efficiently.

5.2 Using Parallel.For and Parallel.ForEach

The Parallel.For and Parallel.ForEach methods enable developers to run loops in parallel, distributing the workload across multiple threads automatically.

5.2.1 Parallel.For

The Parallel.For method allows developers to execute a loop in parallel, improving performance for CPU-bound operations.

```csharp
Copy code
Parallel.For(0, 1000, i =>
{
    // Perform operations in parallel
    Console.WriteLine($"Processing {i} on thread
    {Thread.CurrentThread.ManagedThreadId}");
});
```

5.2.2 Parallel.ForEach

The Parallel.ForEach method operates on collections, allowing developers to process each element in parallel.

74

```csharp
Copy code
var numbers = Enumerable.Range(0, 1000);
Parallel.ForEach(numbers, number =>
{
    Console.WriteLine($"Processing {number} on thread
    {Thread.CurrentThread.ManagedThreadId}");
});
```

5.3 Managing Exceptions in Parallel Loops

When using parallel loops, exceptions can occur in multiple iterations. To handle exceptions properly, developers should use the ParallelLoopResult structure.

```csharp
Copy code
try
{
    Parallel.For(0, 1000, i =>
    {
        if (i == 500) throw new InvalidOperationException("An
        error occurred.");
    });
}
catch (AggregateException ex)
{
    foreach (var innerEx in ex.InnerExceptions)
    {
        Console.WriteLine($"Error: {innerEx.Message}");
    }
}
```

5.4 Parallel LINQ (PLINQ)

Parallel LINQ (PLINQ) extends LINQ by enabling parallel processing of collections. By using PLINQ, developers can write queries that run concurrently, taking advantage of multiple cores.

```csharp
Copy code
var numbers = Enumerable.Range(1, 1000000);

// Perform a parallel LINQ query
var results = numbers.AsParallel()
                  .Where(n => n % 2 == 0)
                  .Select(n => n * n)
                  .ToArray();
```

5.5 Controlling Parallel Execution

PLINQ provides several options for controlling parallel execution, including:

- **WithDegreeOfParallelism**: This option allows developers to specify the maximum degree of parallelism.

```csharp
Copy code
var results = numbers.AsParallel()
                  .WithDegreeOfParallelism(4) // Limit to 4
                  concurrent tasks
                  .Where(n => n % 2 == 0)
                  .Select(n => n * n)
                  .ToArray();
```

- **AsOrdered**: The AsOrdered method can be used to maintain the order of elements.

```csharp
Copy code
var orderedResults = numbers.AsParallel()
                            .AsOrdered()
                            .Where(n => n % 2 == 0)
                            .ToArray();
```

5.6 Best Practices for Parallel Programming

To maximize the benefits of parallel programming in C#, developers should follow these best practices:

- **Identify Parallelizable Workloads**: Before using parallel programming, analyze the workload to determine if it can be effectively divided into independent tasks.
- **Limit Overhead**: Parallelizing small tasks can introduce overhead due to thread management. Ensure that tasks are sufficiently large to justify parallel execution.
- **Avoid Shared State**: Minimize shared state between parallel tasks to reduce the risk of race conditions and the need for synchronization.
- **Use Appropriate Data Structures**: When working with parallel programming, consider using thread-safe collections or data structures that support concurrent access.

Conclusion

The Task Parallel Library (TPL) and asynchronous programming in C# provide powerful tools for developers looking to create responsive and high-performance applications. By leveraging tasks, the async and await keywords, and parallel programming constructs, developers can build applications that take full advantage of modern multi-core processors and asynchronous I/O operations.

Through effective use of TPL, asynchronous programming patterns, and best practices for multithreading and parallel programming, developers can overcome the challenges of high-performance computing and deliver applications that meet the demands of today's users.

As the software landscape continues to evolve, mastering TPL and asynchronous programming will remain essential for developers seeking to create efficient, scalable, and responsive applications. The concepts and techniques discussed in this chapter provide a solid foundation for harnessing the full potential of TPL in high-performance computing scenarios.

4o mini

You said:

write in 7000 words Chapter 7

ChatGPT said:

ChatGPT

Chapter 7: Performance Testing and Benchmarking in .NET 6

In high-performance computing (HPC) and modern application development, ensuring that applications run efficiently and effectively is paramount. Performance testing and benchmarking are essential practices that allow developers to evaluate the speed, scalability, and responsiveness of their applications. This chapter delves into performance testing and benchmarking in .NET 6, exploring tools, techniques, and best practices that can help developers measure and optimize application performance.

1. Introduction to Performance Testing

1.1 What is Performance Testing?

Performance testing is a type of software testing aimed at determining how a system performs under various conditions. It evaluates several performance attributes, including:

- **Response Time**: The time taken for the application to respond to a user request.
- **Throughput**: The number of requests that the application can handle per unit of time.
- **Resource Utilization**: The amount of system resources (CPU, memory, disk, network) consumed during application execution.
- **Scalability**: The application's ability to maintain performance as the load increases.

Performance testing helps identify bottlenecks, scalability issues, and areas for improvement, ensuring that applications can meet user demands.

1.2 Importance of Performance Testing

In today's fast-paced software environment, performance testing is critical for several reasons:

- **User Satisfaction**: Slow applications lead to frustrated users. Performance testing helps ensure applications respond quickly to user interactions, improving user satisfaction and retention.
- **Resource Efficiency**: Efficient applications use fewer resources, reducing operational costs. Performance testing helps identify areas where resource consumption can be optimized.
- **Scalability Assurance**: As applications grow, they must handle increasing loads. Performance testing ensures that applications can scale effectively to accommodate more users and data without degrading performance.

- **Competitive Advantage**: Applications that perform better than competitors can attract more users and gain a competitive edge in the marketplace.

1.3 Types of Performance Testing

Performance testing encompasses various types of tests, each focusing on different aspects of performance:

- **Load Testing**: Simulates the expected load on the application to determine how it behaves under normal and peak conditions.
- **Stress Testing**: Pushes the application beyond its limits to identify breaking points and assess how it recovers from failure.
- **Endurance Testing**: Evaluates how the application performs under sustained load over an extended period to identify issues like memory leaks.
- **Spike Testing**: Tests the application's response to sudden spikes in load to evaluate its ability to handle unexpected traffic.
- **Scalability Testing**: Assesses how the application performs as resources (e.g., hardware, software) are added to accommodate increased loads.

2. Benchmarking in .NET 6

2.1 What is Benchmarking?

Benchmarking is the process of measuring the performance of specific operations or functions within an application. It provides quantitative data that developers can use to compare different implementations or configurations.

2.2 The Importance of Benchmarking

Benchmarking is essential for:

- **Performance Measurement**: It provides precise metrics that help developers understand how different parts of their code perform under various conditions.
- **Optimization Validation**: After implementing optimizations, benchmarking allows developers to measure the impact of changes, ensuring that performance improvements are realized.
- **Comparison of Alternatives**: Benchmarking enables developers to compare different algorithms, libraries, or configurations to identify the most efficient solutions.

2.3 Benchmarking Libraries in .NET

The most widely used library for benchmarking in .NET is **BenchmarkDotNet**. It provides a powerful and easy-to-use framework for measuring the performance of .NET applications.

2.3.1 BenchmarkDotNet Overview

BenchmarkDotNet is an open-source benchmarking library that allows developers to create precise benchmarks for their code. It automates many aspects of the benchmarking process, including:

- Warm-up phases to eliminate JIT compilation and other factors that could skew results.
- Handling of different runtimes and configurations.
- Statistical analysis of benchmark results to ensure accuracy.

2.3.2 Getting Started with BenchmarkDotNet

To use BenchmarkDotNet, you need to install the library via NuGet:

```bash
Copy code
dotnet add package BenchmarkDotNet
```

Once installed, you can create a benchmark class:

```csharp
Copy code
using BenchmarkDotNet.Attributes;
using BenchmarkDotNet.Running;

public class MyBenchmark
{
    [Benchmark]
    public void MyMethod()
    {
        // Code to benchmark
    }
}

public class Program
{
    public static void Main(string[] args)
    {
        BenchmarkRunner.Run<MyBenchmark>();
    }
}
```

In this example, the MyMethod method is marked with the [Benchmark] attribute, indicating that it should be measured. The BenchmarkRunner.Run method executes the benchmark and provides detailed results.

2.4 Analyzing Benchmark Results

BenchmarkDotNet generates comprehensive reports detailing various performance metrics, including:

- **Mean**: The average time taken to execute the benchmarked method.
- **Standard Deviation**: The variability in execution time, indicating the consistency of performance.
- **Throughput**: The number of operations performed per unit of time.

2.5 Best Practices for Benchmarking

To ensure accurate and meaningful benchmarking results, developers should follow best practices:

- **Isolate Benchmarked Code**: Ensure that the code being benchmarked is isolated from other factors that could influence performance, such as global state or shared resources.
- **Warm-Up Iterations**: Include warm-up iterations before measuring to account for JIT compilation and other factors that may affect initial performance.
- **Repeat Benchmarks**: Run benchmarks multiple times to obtain statistically significant results and reduce variability.
- **Analyze Results**: Look for trends in the results and consider using visualizations to communicate findings effectively.

3. Tools for Performance Testing in .NET 6

3.1 Visual Studio Performance Profiler

Visual Studio includes a built-in performance profiler that helps developers analyze application performance. It provides various profiling tools, including CPU usage, memory allocation, and concurrency analysis.

3.1.1 Using the Performance Profiler

To use the performance profiler in Visual Studio:

1. Open your project in Visual Studio.
2. Navigate to Debug > Performance Profiler.

3. Select the profiling tools you wish to use (e.g., CPU Usage, Memory Usage, etc.).
4. Click Start to begin profiling your application.

The performance profiler captures data about your application's execution, allowing you to identify bottlenecks and areas for optimization.

3.2 .NET Benchmarking with BenchmarkDotNet

As discussed earlier, BenchmarkDotNet is an essential tool for benchmarking in .NET. It provides a simple way to measure and compare the performance of methods, enabling developers to optimize code effectively.

3.3 Load Testing Tools

Load testing is critical for assessing how an application performs under varying levels of demand. Several tools can assist with load testing in .NET applications:

- **Apache JMeter**: An open-source load testing tool that allows developers to simulate multiple users and analyze application performance under load.
- **k6**: A modern load testing tool that provides a developer-friendly scripting API and can be integrated into CI/CD pipelines.
- **Artillery**: A powerful, modern, and easy-to-use load testing toolkit designed for testing web applications and APIs.

3.4 Profiling Tools

In addition to Visual Studio's performance profiler, other profiling tools can provide valuable insights into application performance:

- **dotTrace**: A performance profiler from JetBrains that helps analyze CPU usage, memory consumption, and thread activity in .NET applications.

- **PerfView**: A performance analysis tool that collects and analyzes performance data, making it useful for diagnosing performance issues in production applications.
- **Windows Performance Analyzer (WPA)**: A powerful tool for analyzing performance issues on Windows applications, providing detailed insights into CPU, memory, and I/O operations.

4. Implementing Performance Testing Strategies

4.1 Defining Performance Goals

Before conducting performance testing, it is essential to define clear performance goals. These goals should be specific, measurable, and relevant to the application's expected use case. Examples of performance goals include:

- Target response time for API endpoints.
- Maximum acceptable CPU and memory usage during peak load.
- Required throughput (requests per second) for a web application.

4.2 Designing Performance Test Scenarios

To effectively test performance, developers should design scenarios that simulate real-world usage patterns. This involves identifying critical workflows and defining load profiles that reflect expected user behavior.

Key components to consider when designing performance test scenarios include:

- **User Load**: Define the number of users that will be simulated during testing and how they will interact with the application.
- **Test Duration**: Determine the duration of the tests, including ramp-up times and peak load durations.
- **Transaction Mix**: Specify the types of transactions that will be tested

and their expected frequency.

4.3 Executing Performance Tests

Once performance test scenarios are defined, developers can execute tests using the chosen load testing tools. During execution, it is important to monitor key metrics, such as:

- **Response Time**: Measure the time taken for requests to complete.
- **Throughput**: Calculate the number of requests handled per second.
- **Resource Utilization**: Monitor CPU, memory, and disk usage to ensure efficient resource consumption.

4.4 Analyzing Results

After executing performance tests, developers should analyze the results to identify bottlenecks and areas for improvement. Key aspects to consider include:

- **Identifying Bottlenecks**: Look for components or processes that consistently exceed performance goals. This may involve analyzing specific methods, database queries, or external service calls.
- **Comparing Results Against Goals**: Assess whether the application meets the defined performance goals. If not, identify potential optimizations and retest.
- **Trend Analysis**: Track performance over time to identify trends or patterns that may indicate degradation or improvement.

4.5 Continuous Performance Testing

In modern software development, performance testing should be integrated into the CI/CD pipeline to ensure that performance remains a priority throughout the development lifecycle. Continuous performance testing involves:

- **Automating Performance Tests**: Use automation tools to run performance tests regularly, such as during builds or before releases.
- **Monitoring Performance in Production**: Implement application performance monitoring (APM) solutions to track performance in production environments. This allows developers to identify and address performance issues before they impact users.
- **Gathering Feedback**: Collect feedback from performance tests to inform development decisions and prioritize optimization efforts.

5. Best Practices for Performance Testing and Benchmarking

5.1 Documenting Performance Testing

Documentation is essential for performance testing efforts. Maintain clear records of test scenarios, configurations, results, and any identified issues. This documentation serves as a reference for future testing and optimizations.

5.2 Collaborating with Stakeholders

Involve relevant stakeholders, such as developers, QA engineers, and product owners, in the performance testing process. Collaborating ensures that performance goals align with user expectations and business requirements.

5.3 Prioritizing High-Impact Areas

Focus performance testing efforts on high-impact areas of the application, such as critical workflows, frequently used features, or components with known performance issues. This targeted approach ensures that testing is efficient and effective.

5.4 Using Appropriate Testing Tools

Select performance testing tools that align with your application architecture and testing goals. Different tools may be better suited for web applications, APIs, or microservices.

5.5 Iterating on Test Results

Performance testing is an iterative process. After implementing optimizations based on test results, retest the application to validate improvements. Continuously iterate to refine performance and ensure that the application meets evolving user demands.

Conclusion

Performance testing and benchmarking are vital components of developing high-performance applications in .NET 6. By understanding the principles of performance testing, utilizing tools like BenchmarkDotNet, and implementing effective testing strategies, developers can ensure that their applications meet user expectations and deliver a responsive experience.

Incorporating performance testing into the development lifecycle promotes a culture of continuous improvement, enabling developers to identify and address performance issues proactively. As the demands of modern applications continue to grow, mastering performance testing and benchmarking will remain essential for delivering high-quality, efficient software solutions.

Chapter 7: Performance Testing and Benchmarking in .NET 6

I n high-performance computing (HPC) and modern application development, ensuring that applications run efficiently and effectively is paramount. Performance testing and benchmarking are essential practices that allow developers to evaluate the speed, scalability, and responsiveness of their applications. This chapter delves into performance testing and benchmarking in .NET 6, exploring tools, techniques, and best practices that can help developers measure and optimize application performance.

1. Introduction to Performance Testing

1.1 What is Performance Testing?

Performance testing is a type of software testing aimed at determining how a system performs under various conditions. It evaluates several performance attributes, including:

- **Response Time**: The time taken for the application to respond to a user request.
- **Throughput**: The number of requests that the application can handle

per unit of time.

- **Resource Utilization**: The amount of system resources (CPU, memory, disk, network) consumed during application execution.
- **Scalability**: The application's ability to maintain performance as the load increases.

Performance testing helps identify bottlenecks, scalability issues, and areas for improvement, ensuring that applications can meet user demands.

1.2 Importance of Performance Testing

In today's fast-paced software environment, performance testing is critical for several reasons:

- **User Satisfaction**: Slow applications lead to frustrated users. Performance testing helps ensure applications respond quickly to user interactions, improving user satisfaction and retention.
- **Resource Efficiency**: Efficient applications use fewer resources, reducing operational costs. Performance testing helps identify areas where resource consumption can be optimized.
- **Scalability Assurance**: As applications grow, they must handle increasing loads. Performance testing ensures that applications can scale effectively to accommodate more users and data without degrading performance.
- **Competitive Advantage**: Applications that perform better than competitors can attract more users and gain a competitive edge in the marketplace.

1.3 Types of Performance Testing

Performance testing encompasses various types of tests, each focusing on different aspects of performance:

- **Load Testing**: Simulates the expected load on the application to determine how it behaves under normal and peak conditions.
- **Stress Testing**: Pushes the application beyond its limits to identify breaking points and assess how it recovers from failure.
- **Endurance Testing**: Evaluates how the application performs under sustained load over an extended period to identify issues like memory leaks.
- **Spike Testing**: Tests the application's response to sudden spikes in load to evaluate its ability to handle unexpected traffic.
- **Scalability Testing**: Assesses how the application performs as resources (e.g., hardware, software) are added to accommodate increased loads.

2. Benchmarking in .NET 6

2.1 What is Benchmarking?

Benchmarking is the process of measuring the performance of specific operations or functions within an application. It provides quantitative data that developers can use to compare different implementations or configurations.

2.2 The Importance of Benchmarking

Benchmarking is essential for:

- **Performance Measurement**: It provides precise metrics that help developers understand how different parts of their code perform under various conditions.
- **Optimization Validation**: After implementing optimizations, benchmarking allows developers to measure the impact of changes, ensuring that performance improvements are realized.
- **Comparison of Alternatives**: Benchmarking enables developers to compare different algorithms, libraries, or configurations to identify the

most efficient solutions.

2.3 Benchmarking Libraries in .NET

The most widely used library for benchmarking in .NET is **BenchmarkDot-Net**. It provides a powerful and easy-to-use framework for measuring the performance of .NET applications.

2.3.1 BenchmarkDotNet Overview

BenchmarkDotNet is an open-source benchmarking library that allows developers to create precise benchmarks for their code. It automates many aspects of the benchmarking process, including:

- Warm-up phases to eliminate JIT compilation and other factors that could skew results.
- Handling of different runtimes and configurations.
- Statistical analysis of benchmark results to ensure accuracy.

2.3.2 Getting Started with BenchmarkDotNet

To use BenchmarkDotNet, you need to install the library via NuGet:

```bash
Copy code
dotnet add package BenchmarkDotNet
```

Once installed, you can create a benchmark class:

```csharp
Copy code
using BenchmarkDotNet.Attributes;
using BenchmarkDotNet.Running;

public class MyBenchmark
{
```

```
    [Benchmark]
    public void MyMethod()
    {
        // Code to benchmark
    }
}

public class Program
{
    public static void Main(string[] args)
    {
        BenchmarkRunner.Run<MyBenchmark>();
    }
}
```

In this example, the MyMethod method is marked with the [Benchmark] attribute, indicating that it should be measured. The BenchmarkRunner.Run method executes the benchmark and provides detailed results.

2.4 Analyzing Benchmark Results

BenchmarkDotNet generates comprehensive reports detailing various performance metrics, including:

- **Mean**: The average time taken to execute the benchmarked method.
- **Standard Deviation**: The variability in execution time, indicating the consistency of performance.
- **Throughput**: The number of operations performed per unit of time.

2.5 Best Practices for Benchmarking

To ensure accurate and meaningful benchmarking results, developers should follow best practices:

- **Isolate Benchmarked Code**: Ensure that the code being benchmarked is isolated from other factors that could influence performance, such as global state or shared resources.

- **Warm-Up Iterations**: Include warm-up iterations before measuring to account for JIT compilation and other factors that may affect initial performance.
- **Repeat Benchmarks**: Run benchmarks multiple times to obtain statistically significant results and reduce variability.
- **Analyze Results**: Look for trends in the results and consider using visualizations to communicate findings effectively.

3. Tools for Performance Testing in .NET 6

3.1 Visual Studio Performance Profiler

Visual Studio includes a built-in performance profiler that helps developers analyze application performance. It provides various profiling tools, including CPU usage, memory allocation, and concurrency analysis.

3.1.1 Using the Performance Profiler

To use the performance profiler in Visual Studio:

1. Open your project in Visual Studio.
2. Navigate to Debug > Performance Profiler.
3. Select the profiling tools you wish to use (e.g., CPU Usage, Memory Usage, etc.).
4. Click Start to begin profiling your application.

The performance profiler captures data about your application's execution, allowing you to identify bottlenecks and areas for optimization.

3.2 .NET Benchmarking with BenchmarkDotNet

As discussed earlier, BenchmarkDotNet is an essential tool for benchmarking in .NET. It provides a simple way to measure and compare the performance of methods, enabling developers to optimize code effectively.

3.3 Load Testing Tools

Load testing is critical for assessing how an application performs under varying levels of demand. Several tools can assist with load testing in .NET applications:

- **Apache JMeter**: An open-source load testing tool that allows developers to simulate multiple users and analyze application performance under load.
- **k6**: A modern load testing tool that provides a developer-friendly scripting API and can be integrated into CI/CD pipelines.
- **Artillery**: A powerful, modern, and easy-to-use load testing toolkit designed for testing web applications and APIs.

3.4 Profiling Tools

In addition to Visual Studio's performance profiler, other profiling tools can provide valuable insights into application performance:

- **dotTrace**: A performance profiler from JetBrains that helps analyze CPU usage, memory consumption, and thread activity in .NET applications.
- **PerfView**: A performance analysis tool that collects and analyzes performance data, making it useful for diagnosing performance issues in production applications.
- **Windows Performance Analyzer (WPA)**: A powerful tool for analyzing performance issues on Windows applications, providing detailed insights into CPU, memory, and I/O operations.

4. Implementing Performance Testing Strategies

4.1 Defining Performance Goals

Before conducting performance testing, it is essential to define clear performance goals. These goals should be specific, measurable, and relevant to the application's expected use case. Examples of performance goals include:

- Target response time for API endpoints.
- Maximum acceptable CPU and memory usage during peak load.
- Required throughput (requests per second) for a web application.

4.2 Designing Performance Test Scenarios

To effectively test performance, developers should design scenarios that simulate real-world usage patterns. This involves identifying critical workflows and defining load profiles that reflect expected user behavior.

Key components to consider when designing performance test scenarios include:

- **User Load**: Define the number of users that will be simulated during testing and how they will interact with the application.
- **Test Duration**: Determine the duration of the tests, including ramp-up times and peak load durations.
- **Transaction Mix**: Specify the types of transactions that will be tested and their expected frequency.

4.3 Executing Performance Tests

Once performance test scenarios are defined, developers can execute tests using the chosen load testing tools. During execution, it is important to monitor key metrics, such as:

- **Response Time**: Measure the time taken for requests to complete.
- **Throughput**: Calculate the number of requests handled per second.
- **Resource Utilization**: Monitor CPU, memory, and disk usage to ensure efficient resource consumption.

4.4 Analyzing Results

After executing performance tests, developers should analyze the results to identify bottlenecks and areas for improvement. Key aspects to consider include:

- **Identifying Bottlenecks**: Look for components or processes that consistently exceed performance goals. This may involve analyzing specific methods, database queries, or external service calls.
- **Comparing Results Against Goals**: Assess whether the application meets the defined performance goals. If not, identify potential optimizations and retest.
- **Trend Analysis**: Track performance over time to identify trends or patterns that may indicate degradation or improvement.

4.5 Continuous Performance Testing

In modern software development, performance testing should be integrated into the CI/CD pipeline to ensure that performance remains a priority throughout the development lifecycle. Continuous performance testing involves:

- **Automating Performance Tests**: Use automation tools to run performance tests regularly, such as during builds or before releases.
- **Monitoring Performance in Production**: Implement application performance monitoring (APM) solutions to track performance in production environments. This allows developers to identify and address performance issues before they impact users.

- **Gathering Feedback**: Collect feedback from performance tests to inform development decisions and prioritize optimization efforts.

5. Best Practices for Performance Testing and Benchmarking

5.1 Documenting Performance Testing

Documentation is essential for performance testing efforts. Maintain clear records of test scenarios, configurations, results, and any identified issues. This documentation serves as a reference for future testing and optimizations.

5.2 Collaborating with Stakeholders

Involve relevant stakeholders, such as developers, QA engineers, and product owners, in the performance testing process. Collaborating ensures that performance goals align with user expectations and business requirements.

5.3 Prioritizing High-Impact Areas

Focus performance testing efforts on high-impact areas of the application, such as critical workflows, frequently used features, or components with known performance issues. This targeted approach ensures that testing is efficient and effective.

5.4 Using Appropriate Testing Tools

Select performance testing tools that align with your application architecture and testing goals. Different tools may be better suited for web applications, APIs, or microservices.

5.5 Iterating on Test Results

Performance testing is an iterative process. After implementing optimizations based on test results, retest the application to validate improvements. Continuously iterate to refine performance and ensure that the application meets evolving user demands.

Conclusion

Performance testing and benchmarking are vital components of developing high-performance applications in .NET 6. By understanding the principles of performance testing, utilizing tools like BenchmarkDotNet, and implementing effective testing strategies, developers can ensure that their applications meet user expectations and deliver a responsive experience.

Incorporating performance testing into the development lifecycle promotes a culture of continuous improvement, enabling developers to identify and address performance issues proactively. As the demands of modern applications continue to grow, mastering performance testing and benchmarking will remain essential for delivering high-quality, efficient software solutions.

Chapter 8: Memory Management and Optimization Techniques in .NET 6

emory management is a critical aspect of software development, particularly in high-performance applications where efficient resource utilization is essential. In .NET 6, enhancements in memory management provide developers with powerful tools to optimize memory usage and improve application performance. This chapter will explore memory management concepts, techniques for optimizing memory in .NET 6, and best practices for effective memory management.

1. Understanding Memory Management in .NET 6

1.1 Memory Management Overview

Memory management refers to the process of allocating, using, and freeing memory in a software application. It involves managing the memory lifecycle of objects, ensuring that memory is allocated when needed and released when no longer in use. Proper memory management is crucial for maintaining application performance, preventing memory leaks, and ensuring stability.

In .NET, memory management is primarily handled by the Common Language Runtime (CLR), which includes a built-in garbage collector (GC) that automates memory management. The GC tracks object allocations and automatically reclaims memory when objects are no longer accessible.

1.2 The Role of the Garbage Collector

The garbage collector plays a vital role in .NET memory management by performing the following tasks:

- **Memory Allocation**: When an object is created, the garbage collector allocates memory for it on the managed heap.
- **Reference Counting**: The GC keeps track of object references to determine whether an object is still in use. When an object's reference count drops to zero, it is considered unreachable and eligible for garbage collection.
- **Memory Reclamation**: The GC automatically reclaims memory from unreachable objects, freeing up resources for new allocations.

1.3 Generational Garbage Collection

.NET employs a generational garbage collection model, organizing objects into three generations based on their lifetime:

- **Generation 0**: This generation contains newly allocated objects. The garbage collector frequently collects Generation 0 to reclaim memory from short-lived objects.
- **Generation 1**: Objects that survive a Generation 0 collection are promoted to Generation 1. This generation contains objects with a longer lifespan.
- **Generation 2**: Objects that continue to survive collections are promoted to Generation 2, which contains long-lived objects. Collections of Generation 2 are less frequent due to the increased overhead associated with reclaiming memory from this generation.

The generational approach optimizes garbage collection by focusing on short-lived objects that can be quickly reclaimed while reducing the overhead of collecting long-lived objects.

2. Memory Allocation in .NET 6

2.1 Stack vs. Heap Allocation

In .NET, memory allocation can occur on the stack or the heap:

- **Stack Allocation**: Stack allocation is used for value types and method call frames. The stack is a region of memory that operates in a last-in, first-out (LIFO) manner. Stack-allocated memory is automatically released when the method call completes, making it efficient and low-overhead.
- **Heap Allocation**: Heap allocation is used for reference types and dynamic memory allocations. Objects allocated on the heap remain in memory until they are no longer reachable, at which point the garbage collector can reclaim the memory.

2.2 Creating and Managing Objects

When creating objects in .NET, developers can allocate memory on the heap by using reference types. The memory for these objects is managed by the garbage collector.

```csharp
Copy code
public class MyClass
{
    public int MyProperty { get; set; }
}

// Creating an object on the heap
MyClass myObject = new MyClass();
```

In this example, myObject is allocated on the heap, and the memory will be reclaimed by the garbage collector when there are no more references to it.

2.3 Value Types vs. Reference Types

Understanding the difference between value types and reference types is essential for effective memory management in .NET:

- **Value Types**: These types (e.g., structs, enums) are stored directly on the stack or in-line within objects. They have a fixed size and are copied when assigned or passed as parameters. Since they do not require garbage collection, value types are generally more efficient in terms of memory management.
- **Reference Types**: These types (e.g., classes, arrays) are allocated on the heap. When assigned or passed as parameters, only a reference to the object is copied, not the object itself. Reference types require garbage collection, which can introduce overhead.

2.4 Memory Alignment and Padding

Memory alignment refers to the arrangement of data in memory to optimize access speeds. In .NET, the runtime aligns data based on its type, which can lead to padding—unused memory added to ensure proper alignment.

Understanding memory alignment can help developers design more efficient data structures. By organizing data to minimize padding, developers can reduce memory consumption and improve cache locality.

```csharp
Copy code
public struct MyStruct
{
    public int A; // 4 bytes
    public short B; // 2 bytes
    public byte C; // 1 byte
    // Padding added to align the structure to 8 bytes
```

```
}
```

In this example, padding may be added to ensure that the size of MyStruct is a multiple of its alignment requirement.

3. Garbage Collection in .NET 6

3.1 How Garbage Collection Works

The garbage collector in .NET operates through a series of phases to reclaim memory. The primary phases include:

- **Mark Phase**: The GC identifies all live objects by traversing the object graph starting from root references (e.g., global variables, static fields).
- **Sweep Phase**: The GC scans the heap and identifies unreachable objects. These objects are marked for deallocation.
- **Compaction Phase**: To reduce fragmentation, the GC compacts the heap by moving live objects closer together, creating contiguous free space for future allocations.

3.2 Generational Collection

As mentioned earlier, .NET employs generational garbage collection, which optimizes performance by focusing on short-lived objects. The GC frequently collects Generation 0, as most objects in this generation are typically short-lived.

- **Minor Collection**: This refers to the collection of Generation 0. It is performed more frequently to quickly reclaim memory from short-lived objects.
- **Major Collection**: This refers to the collection of Generations 1 and 2. It occurs less frequently due to the increased overhead and is typically triggered when the heap usage reaches a certain threshold.

3.3 Triggering Garbage Collection

Developers can manually trigger garbage collection using the GC.Collect method. However, this is generally discouraged unless absolutely necessary, as the GC is designed to operate automatically and efficiently.

```csharp
Copy code
GC.Collect(); // Manually trigger garbage collection
```

Instead, developers should focus on writing code that allows the garbage collector to operate effectively without intervention.

3.4 Performance Impact of Garbage Collection

Garbage collection can impact application performance, particularly during collection cycles. GC pauses may lead to latency in applications, affecting user experience. To mitigate these impacts, developers can:

- **Reduce Allocations**: Minimize the number of allocations and deallocations to reduce the workload on the garbage collector.
- **Optimize Object Lifetimes**: Design objects with appropriate lifetimes to ensure that short-lived objects are quickly collected, and long-lived objects remain available without frequent collections.
- **Use Object Pools**: Implement object pooling for frequently created and destroyed objects to reduce the frequency of heap allocations and deallocations.

3.5 Configuring Garbage Collection

In .NET 6, developers can configure garbage collection settings to optimize performance based on application needs. Key configurations include:

- **Server vs. Workstation Mode**: The garbage collector can operate in either server mode (optimized for high-throughput applications) or workstation mode (optimized for low-latency applications). Developers can configure this in the application's configuration file.
- **Concurrent Garbage Collection**: Enabling concurrent garbage collection allows the GC to run in the background while the application continues executing, reducing the impact of GC pauses.
- **Low-Latency Mode**: Applications that require low-latency behavior can configure the garbage collector to enter low-latency mode, minimizing the frequency and duration of collections.

4. Optimizing Memory Usage in .NET 6

4.1 Object Lifetime Management

Managing the lifetime of objects is crucial for effective memory optimization. Developers can implement strategies to ensure that objects are disposed of properly when they are no longer needed:

- **Implementing IDisposable**: Classes that hold unmanaged resources (e.g., file handles, database connections) should implement the IDisposable interface to provide a way to release resources explicitly.

```csharp
Copy code
public class MyClass : IDisposable
{
    private bool disposed = false;

    public void Dispose()
    {
        Dispose(true);
        GC.SuppressFinalize(this);
```

```csharp
    }

    protected virtual void Dispose(bool disposing)
    {
        if (!disposed)
        {
            if (disposing)
            {
                // Release managed resources
            }
            // Release unmanaged resources
            disposed = true;
        }
    }

    ~MyClass()
    {
        Dispose(false); // Finalizer calls Dispose
    }
}
```

- **Using the using Statement**: The using statement provides a convenient syntax for ensuring that objects are disposed of automatically when they go out of scope.

```csharp
csharp
Copy code
using (var myObject = new MyClass())
{
    // Use myObject
} // Automatically calls Dispose at the end of the block
```

4.2 Reducing Heap Allocations

Reducing the number of heap allocations is one of the most effective ways to optimize memory usage in .NET applications. Strategies for minimizing heap allocations include:

- **Object Pooling**: Implementing object pooling allows frequently used objects to be reused instead of constantly allocating and deallocating memory.

```csharp
Copy code
public class ObjectPool<T> where T : new()
{
    private readonly Stack<T> _pool = new Stack<T>();

    public T Get()
    {
        return _pool.Count > 0 ? _pool.Pop() : new T();
    }

    public void Return(T item)
    {
        _pool.Push(item);
    }
}
```

- **Using Structs Instead of Classes**: For small, immutable types, consider using structs (value types) instead of classes (reference types) to reduce heap allocations. Structs are allocated on the stack and have lower overhead.

4.3 Memory Profiling and Analysis

To optimize memory usage effectively, developers should profile and analyze their applications. Tools for memory profiling in .NET include:

- **Visual Studio Diagnostic Tools**: Visual Studio includes built-in diagnostic tools that allow developers to analyze memory usage, identify memory leaks, and examine the object heap.
- **dotMemory**: A powerful memory profiler from JetBrains that provides detailed insights into memory usage, object allocation, and potential leaks.
- **PerfView**: A performance analysis tool that captures memory allocation events and helps identify problematic areas in applications.

4.4 Memory-Mapped Files and Buffers

In scenarios where large datasets need to be accessed efficiently, developers can use memory-mapped files and buffers to optimize memory usage:

- **Memory-Mapped Files**: Memory-mapped files allow developers to map the contents of a file directly into memory, enabling fast access without the need to load the entire file into memory. This is particularly useful for large files or databases.

```csharp
Copy code
using (var mmf = MemoryMappedFile.CreateNew("testmap", 10000))
{
    using (var stream = mmf.CreateViewStream())
    {
        // Write or read from the memory-mapped file
    }
}
```

- **Span\<T\> and Memory\<T\>**: Use Span\<T\> and Memory\<T\> for efficient memory management when working with slices of data, as these types allow developers to manipulate memory without incurring the overhead of heap allocations.

```csharp
Copy code
Span<byte> buffer = stackalloc byte[256]; // Allocated on the stack
```

4.5 Leveraging Native Memory Allocations

For performance-critical applications, developers can leverage native memory allocations to manage memory outside the managed heap. This allows for more granular control over memory usage:

- **Marshal Class**: The Marshal class provides methods for allocating and freeing unmanaged memory.

```csharp
Copy code
IntPtr unmanagedMemory = Marshal.AllocHGlobal(size); // Allocate
unmanaged memory
try
{
    // Use unmanaged memory
}
finally
{
    Marshal.FreeHGlobal(unmanagedMemory); // Free unmanaged memory
}
```

4.6 Understanding the Large Object Heap (LOH)

The Large Object Heap (LOH) is a special section of the managed heap used to store objects larger than 85,000 bytes. Understanding the LOH is crucial for optimizing memory usage in applications that frequently allocate large objects.

- **Fragmentation Issues**: The LOH is prone to fragmentation due to the allocation and deallocation of large objects. To mitigate fragmentation, consider using object pooling or breaking large objects into smaller chunks.
- **Manual LOH Compaction**: In .NET 6, developers can manually trigger LOH compaction by configuring the garbage collector settings, allowing for more efficient memory usage in scenarios with high LOH fragmentation.

5. Best Practices for Memory Management in .NET 6

5.1 Monitor Memory Usage

Regularly monitor memory usage in production applications to identify potential issues. Use performance monitoring tools to track memory allocation patterns, garbage collection events, and memory leaks.

5.2 Optimize Object Lifetimes

Design objects with appropriate lifetimes to ensure they are released when no longer needed. Implement IDisposable for classes that hold unmanaged resources and use the using statement to automatically dispose of them.

5.3 Reduce Allocations

Minimize memory allocations by using value types where appropriate, implementing object pooling, and avoiding excessive temporary object creation.

5.4 Use Efficient Data Structures

Select data structures that are optimized for the specific use case. Consider using collections from the System.Collections.Concurrent namespace for thread-safe operations, or use arrays for fixed-size collections to reduce overhead.

5.5 Implement Memory Profiling

Incorporate memory profiling into the development lifecycle to identify memory-related issues early in the process. Regularly analyze memory usage to ensure that optimizations are effective.

5.6 Educate the Team

Ensure that all team members understand the principles of memory management and optimization in .NET. Provide training and resources to help developers write efficient, high-performance code.

Conclusion

Memory management is a critical aspect of application development in .NET 6, particularly in high-performance computing scenarios. By understanding the principles of memory management, leveraging the capabilities of the garbage collector, and implementing effective optimization techniques, developers can create efficient, responsive applications that meet the demands of today's users.

This chapter explored various aspects of memory management in .NET 6, including memory allocation, garbage collection, and optimization strategies. By applying the best practices outlined in this chapter, developers can ensure that their applications use memory effectively, improve performance, and enhance overall user experience.

As the software landscape continues to evolve, mastering memory management and optimization will remain essential for developers seeking to build high-performance applications that stand out in an increasingly competitive environment. By prioritizing memory efficiency and leveraging the features of .NET 6, developers can deliver applications that not only meet performance expectations but also provide a seamless user experience.

Chapter 9: Advanced Performance Optimization Techniques in .NET 6

As applications grow in complexity and scale, optimizing performance becomes increasingly important. High-performance computing (HPC) requires not only a solid understanding of the underlying architecture and programming paradigms but also the ability to apply advanced optimization techniques effectively. This chapter explores various advanced performance optimization strategies in .NET 6, including code optimization, concurrency patterns, efficient data management, and profiling techniques that can help developers achieve maximum performance in their applications.

1. Understanding Performance Optimization

1.1 What is Performance Optimization?

Performance optimization is the process of improving the efficiency of an application to ensure it operates at its best under various conditions. It involves analyzing the application's performance metrics, identifying bottlenecks, and implementing changes to enhance speed, responsiveness, and resource utilization. In the context of .NET 6, performance optimization encompasses a wide range of techniques and practices aimed at maximizing the capabilities of the .NET runtime and the underlying hardware.

1.2 The Importance of Performance Optimization

In today's software landscape, performance optimization is critical for several reasons:

- **User Experience**: Fast and responsive applications lead to increased user satisfaction. Users are more likely to continue using applications that perform well.
- **Resource Efficiency**: Optimized applications consume fewer system resources, resulting in lower operational costs and improved scalability.
- **Competitive Advantage**: In a crowded marketplace, applications that offer superior performance can attract and retain more users.

1.3 Performance Optimization Goals

When optimizing performance, it's important to set clear goals that align with the needs of the application and its users. Common goals for performance optimization include:

- **Reducing Response Time**: Ensuring that the application responds quickly to user inputs and requests.
- **Increasing Throughput**: Maximizing the number of operations completed per unit of time, particularly in high-load scenarios.
- **Minimizing Resource Utilization**: Reducing CPU, memory, and I/O usage to improve efficiency and lower costs.
- **Ensuring Scalability**: Making sure the application can handle increasing loads without degrading performance.

2. Code Optimization Techniques

2.1 Efficient Algorithms and Data Structures

Choosing the right algorithms and data structures is crucial for optimizing performance. An inefficient algorithm can lead to unnecessary resource consumption, while the wrong data structure can slow down access times.

2.1.1 Analyzing Algorithm Complexity

When optimizing code, it's essential to analyze the time and space complexity of algorithms using Big O notation. This analysis helps identify potential performance issues.

- **Time Complexity**: Indicates how the execution time of an algorithm grows with the size of the input. For example, a linear search has a time complexity of $O(n)$, while a binary search has a time complexity of $O(\log n)$.
- **Space Complexity**: Indicates how the memory consumption of an algorithm grows with the size of the input.

When selecting an algorithm, prefer those with lower time complexity for performance-critical operations.

2.1.2 Choosing Appropriate Data Structures

Using the right data structures can significantly impact performance. In .NET, various built-in data structures are available, each with its performance characteristics:

- **Arrays**: Fixed-size collections with fast access times. Ideal for scenarios where the size of the collection is known and does not change.
- **Lists**: Dynamic collections that allow for resizing. List<T> is a commonly used collection in .NET for scenarios where frequent insertions and deletions are expected.
- **Dictionaries**: Hash-based collections that provide fast lookups. Use Dictionary<TKey, TValue> for scenarios where key-value pairs are needed.
- **Concurrent Collections**: Thread-safe collections such as ConcurrentD

ictionary, ConcurrentQueue, and BlockingCollection are designed for concurrent access, making them suitable for multithreaded applications.

2.2 Minimizing Method Call Overhead

Method calls, especially when they involve significant overhead (such as virtual calls), can slow down performance. To minimize this overhead:

- **Use Value Types**: Value types (structs) have lower method call overhead compared to reference types (classes). When possible, use value types for small, immutable data structures.
- **Inline Small Methods**: For small methods that are called frequently, consider inlining them to eliminate the overhead associated with the method call.
- **Reduce Virtual Calls**: Virtual method calls introduce additional overhead. If possible, use concrete classes to avoid virtual dispatch.

2.3 Compiler Optimizations

The .NET runtime and the Just-In-Time (JIT) compiler perform various optimizations that can improve performance. Developers can take advantage of these optimizations by:

- **Enabling Release Builds**: Always run performance tests on release builds, as they include optimizations that are not present in debug builds.
- **Using the AggressiveInlining Attribute**: Mark methods with the [MethodImpl(MethodImplOptions.AggressiveInlining)] attribute to encourage the compiler to inline the method, reducing the overhead of the method call.

2.4 Loop Optimization Techniques

Loops are often critical performance hotspots. To optimize loops, consider the following techniques:

2.4.1 Unrolling Loops

Loop unrolling is a technique that involves expanding the loop body to reduce the overhead of loop control and increase the efficiency of the loop. This is particularly effective for small, fixed-size loops.

```csharp
Copy code
// Traditional loop
for (int i = 0; i < 4; i++)
{
    ProcessItem(i);
}

// Unrolled loop
ProcessItem(0);
ProcessItem(1);
ProcessItem(2);
ProcessItem(3);
```

2.4.2 Using Parallel Loops

For CPU-bound tasks, using parallel loops can significantly improve performance. The Parallel.For and Parallel.ForEach methods in TPL allow developers to execute loops in parallel, distributing the workload across multiple threads.

```csharp
Copy code
Parallel.For(0, 1000, i =>
{
    ProcessItem(i);
});
```

2.5 Caching and Memoization

Caching results can improve performance, especially for expensive computations or I/O operations. Memoization is a specific form of caching that
stores the results of expensive function calls and returns the cached result
when the same inputs occur again.

```csharp
Copy code
private readonly Dictionary<int, int> _cache = new Dictionary<int,
int>();

public int ExpensiveCalculation(int input)
{
    if (_cache.TryGetValue(input, out int result))
    {
        return result; // Return cached result
    }

    result = Calculate(input); // Perform the expensive calculation
    _cache[input] = result; // Cache the result
    return result;
}
```

3. Concurrency Patterns in .NET 6

3.1 Introduction to Concurrency Patterns

Concurrency patterns are established solutions for common problems that
arise in concurrent programming. In .NET, several concurrency patterns can
be leveraged to enhance performance and improve resource utilization.

3.2 Producer-Consumer Pattern

The producer-consumer pattern is a classic concurrency pattern where producers generate data and place it in a shared buffer, while consumers retrieve and process that data. This pattern can be implemented using BlockingCollection<T>, which provides a thread-safe collection that handles synchronization.

```csharp
Copy code
BlockingCollection<int> queue = new BlockingCollection<int>();

// Producer
Task.Run(() =>
{
    for (int i = 0; i < 100; i++)
    {
        queue.Add(i); // Add items to the queue
    }
    queue.CompleteAdding(); // Mark the collection as complete
});

// Consumer
Task.Run(() =>
{
    foreach (var item in queue.GetConsumingEnumerable())
    {
        ProcessItem(item); // Process items from the queue
    }
});
```

3.3 Task-Based Asynchronous Pattern

The task-based asynchronous pattern uses tasks to represent asynchronous operations. This pattern allows developers to write non-blocking code and manage concurrency efficiently.

```csharp
csharp
Copy code
public async Task ProcessDataAsync()
{
    var tasks = new List<Task>
    {
        GetDataAsync(),
        GetDataAsync(),
        GetDataAsync()
    };
    await Task.WhenAll(tasks); // Wait for all tasks to complete
}
```

3.4 Fork/Join Pattern

The fork/join pattern is used for parallel processing by dividing a task into subtasks (forking) and then combining the results (joining). This pattern can be implemented using TPL's Parallel.Invoke method.

```csharp
csharp
Copy code
Parallel.Invoke(
    () => ProcessDataPart1(),
    () => ProcessDataPart2(),
    () => ProcessDataPart3()
);
```

3.5 Async/Await and Concurrency

The async and await keywords simplify the implementation of asynchronous operations while allowing concurrent execution. This pattern is essential for writing responsive applications that perform I/O-bound tasks without blocking the main thread.

```csharp
Copy code
public async Task<int> FetchDataAsync()
{
    var data1 = await GetDataFromSource1Async();
    var data2 = await GetDataFromSource2Async();
    return data1 + data2;
}
```

4. Efficient Data Management Techniques

4.1 Memory Allocation Strategies

Efficient memory allocation strategies are crucial for optimizing performance in .NET applications. Developers can adopt the following strategies to minimize memory allocations:

4.1.1 Object Pooling

Object pooling is a technique that allows the reuse of objects instead of creating new instances. This reduces the overhead of memory allocation and garbage collection.

```csharp
Copy code
public class ObjectPool<T> where T : new()
{
    private readonly Stack<T> _pool = new Stack<T>();

    public T Get()
    {
        return _pool.Count > 0 ? _pool.Pop() : new T();
    }

    public void Return(T item)
    {
```

```
        _pool.Push(item);
    }
}
```

4.1.2 Using Span<T> and Memory<T>

In .NET 6, Span<T> and Memory<T> provide a way to manage memory more efficiently. These types allow developers to work with slices of memory without incurring the overhead of heap allocations.

```csharp
Copy code
Span<int> span = stackalloc int[10]; // Allocated on the stack
```

4.2 Data Serialization Optimization

When transferring data between systems or saving it to disk, serialization can introduce performance overhead. To optimize data serialization:

- **Use Efficient Formats**: Choose serialization formats that offer better performance and smaller payload sizes, such as Protocol Buffers or MessagePack, instead of JSON or XML.
- **Minimize Object Creation**: When deserializing data, use techniques that minimize object creation, such as using Span<T> for buffering during the deserialization process.

4.3 Data Caching

Caching frequently accessed data can improve performance significantly. Implement caching strategies to store results of expensive operations or data retrieval.

- **In-Memory Caching**: Use in-memory caching for data that needs to be accessed frequently. Libraries like **MemoryCache** can help implement this.

```csharp
Copy code
var cache = new MemoryCache(new MemoryCacheOptions());
var data = cache.GetOrCreate("key", entry =>
{
    entry.AbsoluteExpirationRelativeToNow =
    TimeSpan.FromMinutes(5);
    return ExpensiveDataRetrieval();
});
```

- **Distributed Caching**: For applications that scale across multiple servers, consider using distributed caching solutions like Redis or Azure Cache for Redis.

5. Profiling and Analyzing Performance

5.1 The Importance of Profiling

Profiling is the process of analyzing an application's performance to identify bottlenecks and areas for optimization. Effective profiling allows developers to make informed decisions about where to focus optimization efforts.

5.2 Profiling Tools in .NET 6

Several profiling tools are available for .NET applications, each offering different capabilities:

- **Visual Studio Diagnostic Tools**: The built-in diagnostic tools in Visual Studio allow developers to profile CPU usage, memory allocations, and more.

- **dotTrace**: A performance profiler from JetBrains that provides detailed insights into CPU and memory usage, enabling developers to identify hotspots in their applications.
- **PerfView**: A powerful performance analysis tool that collects performance data and provides deep insights into application behavior.

5.3 Analyzing Profiling Data

When analyzing profiling data, focus on identifying key performance metrics, including:

- **CPU Usage**: Look for methods or operations that consume excessive CPU time. Optimize these hotspots to improve overall performance.
- **Memory Allocations**: Identify areas of the code that allocate memory frequently or excessively. Consider using object pooling or optimizing data structures to reduce allocations.
- **Garbage Collection**: Analyze garbage collection behavior to identify potential memory leaks or excessive GC activity that may impact performance.

5.4 Continuous Profiling

Incorporating continuous profiling into the development process allows teams to monitor performance changes over time. This can help catch performance regressions early and ensure that optimizations remain effective as the application evolves.

6. Best Practices for Performance Optimization in .NET 6

6.1 Profile Before Optimizing

Before making optimizations, always profile the application to identify performance bottlenecks. Focus on optimizing areas with the most significant impact on performance rather than guessing where problems may lie.

6.2 Measure and Validate Improvements

After implementing optimizations, measure the performance impact to validate the effectiveness of changes. Use benchmarking and profiling tools to gather metrics before and after optimizations.

6.3 Document Optimization Decisions

Keep clear documentation of performance optimization decisions, including the rationale behind each change and the metrics used to measure success. This documentation will serve as a reference for future development and maintenance.

6.4 Keep Code Maintainable

While optimizing performance is essential, ensure that code remains maintainable and readable. Optimize only where necessary and consider the trade-off between performance and code complexity.

6.5 Stay Updated on Best Practices

The .NET ecosystem is continuously evolving. Stay informed about new features, tools, and best practices for performance optimization by following the official .NET documentation and community resources.

Conclusion

Advanced performance optimization techniques in .NET 6 empower developers to create high-performance applications that meet the demands of users and the complexities of modern computing. By understanding memory management, utilizing efficient algorithms and data structures, leveraging concurrency patterns, and employing profiling tools, developers can optimize their applications for speed, responsiveness, and resource efficiency.

This chapter explored a wide range of optimization techniques, including code optimization strategies, concurrency patterns, efficient data management, and profiling methods. By applying the principles and practices discussed in this chapter, developers can enhance their skills in performance optimization, leading to the creation of robust, high-performance applications that excel in today's competitive software landscape.

Chapter 10: Building Scalable Applications with .NET 6

As applications evolve to meet increasing user demands and complexity, scalability becomes a crucial aspect of software design. A scalable application can accommodate growth—whether in terms of user traffic, data volume, or feature complexity—without sacrificing performance. In this chapter, we will explore the principles of building scalable applications using .NET 6, covering architectural patterns, design principles, and practical implementation strategies that can help developers create systems capable of handling future growth.

1. Understanding Scalability

1.1 What is Scalability?

Scalability is the ability of an application to handle increased load or demand without degrading performance. It refers to the capacity of the system to grow and adapt as needed, ensuring that it can support a growing number of users, transactions, or data without requiring a complete redesign.

1.2 Types of Scalability

There are two primary types of scalability:

- **Vertical Scalability (Scaling Up)**: This involves increasing the resources (CPU, memory, storage) of a single server to improve its performance. While vertical scaling can be effective, it has limitations due to hardware constraints and may lead to a single point of failure.
- **Horizontal Scalability (Scaling Out)**: This involves adding more servers or instances to distribute the load across multiple machines. Horizontal scaling provides better fault tolerance, as the failure of one instance does not affect the entire system.

1.3 The Importance of Scalability

Building scalable applications is essential for several reasons:

- **Handling Growth**: As user traffic increases, a scalable application can accommodate the additional load without performance degradation.
- **Cost Efficiency**: Scalable applications can optimize resource usage, reducing operational costs by only using additional resources when necessary.
- **Future-Proofing**: Building scalability into the architecture ensures that the application can evolve to meet future demands without requiring a complete overhaul.

2. Architectural Patterns for Scalability

2.1 Microservices Architecture

Microservices architecture is a popular approach to building scalable applications. It involves breaking an application into smaller, loosely coupled services, each responsible for a specific business function.

2.1.1 Benefits of Microservices

- **Independent Deployment**: Each microservice can be developed, deployed, and scaled independently, allowing for faster release cycles and reduced downtime.
- **Technology Agnosticism**: Different microservices can use different technologies and languages, enabling teams to choose the best tools for their specific tasks.
- **Resilience**: The failure of one microservice does not impact the entire application, improving fault tolerance.

2.1.2 Challenges of Microservices

While microservices offer many benefits, they also introduce complexity, including:

- **Increased Operational Overhead**: Managing multiple services requires sophisticated deployment and orchestration strategies.
- **Data Management**: Ensuring data consistency across microservices can be challenging, especially in distributed systems.
- **Network Latency**: Communication between microservices over the network can introduce latency compared to in-process calls.

2.2 Serverless Architecture

Serverless architecture abstracts the underlying infrastructure, allowing developers to focus on writing code without managing servers. In a serverless model, the cloud provider automatically handles resource allocation and scaling.

2.2.1 Benefits of Serverless Architecture

- **Automatic Scaling**: Serverless applications automatically scale based on demand, ensuring optimal resource usage.
- **Cost Efficiency**: You pay only for the compute resources used during

execution, reducing costs for low-traffic applications.

- **Faster Development**: Developers can focus on building features rather than managing infrastructure.

2.2.2 Limitations of Serverless Architecture

Despite its advantages, serverless architecture has some limitations:

- **Cold Start Latency**: Functions that are not actively running may experience latency when invoked for the first time.
- **Vendor Lock-In**: Serverless solutions can tie applications to specific cloud providers, making migration difficult.

2.3 Event-Driven Architecture

Event-driven architecture is a design pattern that uses events as the primary means of communication between services. In this model, services react to events generated by other services or systems.

2.3.1 Benefits of Event-Driven Architecture

- **Loose Coupling**: Services are decoupled, allowing them to evolve independently and reducing the impact of changes.
- **Asynchronous Processing**: Event-driven systems can handle high volumes of events asynchronously, improving responsiveness.
- **Scalability**: By using message brokers or event streaming platforms, systems can scale by distributing event processing across multiple instances.

2.3.2 Considerations for Event-Driven Architecture

While event-driven architecture offers scalability and flexibility, it also introduces challenges:

- **Complexity**: Managing events and ensuring consistency across distributed services can be complex.

- **Eventual Consistency**: Achieving consistency in an event-driven system may require careful design, as data may not be immediately consistent across services.

3. Design Principles for Scalable Applications

3.1 Loose Coupling

Design systems with loose coupling to minimize dependencies between components. This allows individual components to be modified, replaced, or scaled independently.

3.2 High Cohesion

Ensure that related functionality is grouped together within components or services. High cohesion improves maintainability and makes it easier to understand the system.

3.3 Statelessness

Aim to keep services stateless whenever possible. Stateless services do not store information about previous interactions, making them easier to scale and manage.

3.4 Load Balancing

Implement load balancing to distribute incoming requests evenly across multiple instances of services. Load balancers help prevent any single instance from becoming a bottleneck.

3.5 Caching Strategies

Incorporate caching strategies to reduce latency and improve performance. Caching frequently accessed data can significantly reduce the load on databases and services.

3.6 Data Partitioning

Use data partitioning (sharding) to distribute data across multiple databases or instances. This helps improve scalability and performance by reducing contention for resources.

4. Implementing Scalability in .NET 6

4.1 ASP.NET Core for Web Applications

ASP.NET Core is a powerful framework for building scalable web applications. Key features that enhance scalability include:

4.1.1 Middleware Pipeline

ASP.NET Core uses a middleware pipeline to handle HTTP requests. Developers can add middleware components to process requests and responses, allowing for modular design and separation of concerns.

4.1.2 Dependency Injection

ASP.NET Core has built-in support for dependency injection (DI), promoting loose coupling and testability. Using DI allows for easy substitution of services, making it simpler to implement scalable architectures.

4.1.3 Asynchronous Controllers

ASP.NET Core supports asynchronous action methods in controllers, enabling non-blocking processing of requests. This is particularly useful for I/O-bound operations, allowing the server to handle more concurrent requests.

```csharp
Copy code
public async Task<IActionResult> GetDataAsync()
{
    var data = await _dataService.GetDataAsync();
    return Ok(data);
}
```

4.2 Leveraging Cloud Services

When building scalable applications, consider leveraging cloud services that provide auto-scaling, managed databases, and other features that simplify scaling.

4.2.1 Azure App Services

Azure App Services allows developers to deploy and scale web applications easily. Auto-scaling features can automatically adjust the number of instances based on traffic patterns.

4.2.2 Azure Functions

Azure Functions provides a serverless computing platform that enables developers to run event-driven code without managing infrastructure. Functions can automatically scale based on demand, making them ideal for burst workloads.

4.2.3 Azure Cosmos DB

Azure Cosmos DB is a globally distributed, multi-model database service that offers automatic scaling and low-latency access to data. Its design supports horizontal scaling, making it suitable for applications with large datasets.

4.3 Implementing Asynchronous Processing

Asynchronous processing is crucial for building scalable applications, especially in scenarios involving I/O operations. Use asynchronous programming techniques to prevent blocking calls.

4.3.1 Background Services

In ASP.NET Core, background services can be implemented using the IHostedService interface. Background services run in the background and can process long-running tasks without blocking the main application.

```csharp
Copy code
public class MyBackgroundService : BackgroundService
{
    protected override async Task ExecuteAsync(CancellationToken
    stoppingToken)
    {
        while (!stoppingToken.IsCancellationRequested)
        {
            // Perform background processing
            await Task.Delay(TimeSpan.FromSeconds(5),
            stoppingToken);
        }
    }
}
```

4.3.2 Queuing Mechanisms

Implement queuing mechanisms to decouple components and allow for asynchronous processing. Use message brokers such as Azure Service Bus, RabbitMQ, or AWS SQS to handle communication between services.

5. Testing Scalability and Performance

5.1 Load Testing

Load testing is essential for verifying the scalability of applications. Simulate user traffic to evaluate how the application behaves under expected and peak loads.

5.1.1 Load Testing Tools

Several tools can assist with load testing .NET applications:

- **Apache JMeter**: An open-source load testing tool that allows developers to create and run performance tests.
- **k6**: A modern load testing tool designed for ease of use and integration into CI/CD pipelines.
- **Artillery**: A powerful, easy-to-use load testing toolkit for testing web applications and APIs.

5.2 Stress Testing

Stress testing pushes applications beyond normal operational capacity to identify breaking points and evaluate how the system recovers from failure.

5.2.1 Designing Stress Tests

When designing stress tests, consider the following:

- **Simulate Extreme Loads**: Generate traffic levels significantly higher than expected peak loads to evaluate the system's resilience.
- **Monitor System Health**: Track key performance metrics (CPU, memory, response times) during stress tests to identify potential issues.
- **Evaluate Recovery Strategies**: Assess how the application handles failures and recovers after stress conditions.

5.3 Monitoring and Observability

Effective monitoring and observability are essential for maintaining scalability. Implement logging and monitoring solutions to track application performance and identify issues in real-time.

5.3.1 Application Insights

Azure Application Insights provides powerful monitoring and analytics capabilities for .NET applications. It offers features such as:

- **Performance Metrics**: Track response times, failure rates, and other key performance indicators.
- **Dependency Tracking**: Monitor external dependencies (e.g., databases,

services) to identify bottlenecks.

- **Live Metrics Stream**: View real-time performance metrics to quickly diagnose issues as they arise.

5.4 Continuous Integration and Continuous Deployment (CI/CD)

Integrating scalability testing into the CI/CD pipeline ensures that performance remains a priority throughout the development lifecycle. Automated testing can help catch performance regressions early.

5.4.1 Implementing CI/CD for .NET Applications

Use CI/CD tools such as Azure DevOps, GitHub Actions, or Jenkins to automate the build, test, and deployment process for .NET applications.

- **Automated Load Testing**: Incorporate automated load tests into the CI/CD pipeline to ensure that performance is validated with every code change.
- **Environment Consistency**: Use containerization (e.g., Docker) to ensure consistency across development, testing, and production environments.

6. Conclusion

Building scalable applications in .NET 6 requires a comprehensive understanding of architectural patterns, design principles, and practical implementation strategies. By leveraging the capabilities of .NET 6, including ASP.NET Core for web applications, cloud services for auto-scaling, and asynchronous processing techniques, developers can create systems that effectively handle increasing user demands.

This chapter explored various approaches to scalability, including microservices architecture, serverless computing, and event-driven architecture. We also discussed essential design principles, efficient data management techniques, and testing strategies to ensure that applications remain performant as they scale.

As the landscape of software development continues to evolve, mastering scalability principles and practices will empower developers to build robust applications that meet the challenges of tomorrow. By prioritizing scalability in the design and implementation of applications, developers can create systems that are not only capable of handling current loads but also adaptable to future growth, ensuring sustained performance and user satisfaction.

Chapter 11: Security Considerations in High-Performance Applications with .NET 6

A s applications become more sophisticated and interconnected, the importance of security cannot be overstated. In high-performance computing (HPC) and application development, ensuring that security measures do not impede performance while still providing robust protection is a critical challenge. This chapter will explore security considerations specific to .NET 6 applications, covering authentication and authorization mechanisms, secure coding practices, data protection, and the integration of security into the application lifecycle.

1. Understanding Security in High-Performance Applications

1.1 The Need for Security

Security is a fundamental aspect of software development, particularly for applications handling sensitive data or critical operations. Threats such as data breaches, unauthorized access, and denial-of-service attacks can have severe consequences, including financial loss, reputational damage, and legal repercussions.

1.2 The Balance Between Security and Performance

In high-performance applications, there is often a trade-off between security measures and application performance. Security features such as encryption, authentication, and logging can introduce overhead, potentially impacting response times and throughput. Therefore, it is essential to implement security in a way that minimizes performance impacts while maintaining robust protections.

1.3 Key Security Principles

When designing secure applications, developers should adhere to several key principles:

- **Least Privilege**: Grant users and components the minimum permissions necessary to perform their functions. This reduces the risk of unauthorized access and limits potential damage in case of a breach.
- **Defense in Depth**: Implement multiple layers of security controls to protect against different types of threats. This approach ensures that if one layer fails, additional layers can provide protection.
- **Secure by Design**: Incorporate security considerations into the design phase of development rather than treating it as an afterthought. This proactive approach helps identify potential vulnerabilities early in the process.

2. Authentication and Authorization in .NET 6

2.1 Authentication vs. Authorization

Before diving into security mechanisms, it is crucial to understand the distinction between authentication and authorization:

- **Authentication**: The process of verifying the identity of a user or system.

This can be achieved through various methods, such as usernames and passwords, tokens, or biometrics.

- **Authorization**: The process of determining whether an authenticated user has permission to access specific resources or perform certain actions.

2.2 Authentication Mechanisms in .NET 6

.NET 6 offers several authentication mechanisms that can be integrated into applications, including:

2.2.1 ASP.NET Core Identity

ASP.NET Core Identity is a membership system that provides authentication and authorization services for web applications. It includes features for managing user accounts, roles, and claims-based authentication.

- **User Registration and Management**: ASP.NET Core Identity provides built-in functionality for user registration, password recovery, and account management.
- **Claims-Based Authentication**: Users can be assigned claims (key-value pairs) that represent their permissions or roles within the application. This allows for flexible authorization models.

2.2.2 JWT Bearer Authentication

JSON Web Tokens (JWT) are a popular method for implementing stateless authentication in web applications. JWTs are compact, URL-safe tokens that contain claims and are signed by a secret or public/private key pair.

- **Implementing JWT Authentication**: To use JWT in an ASP.NET Core application, developers can configure authentication middleware in the Startup.cs file.

```csharp
Copy code
public void ConfigureServices(IServiceCollection services)
{
    services.AddAuthentication(JwtBearerDefaults.AuthenticationScheme)
        .AddJwtBearer(options =>
        {
            options.TokenValidationParameters = new
            TokenValidationParameters
            {
                ValidateIssuer = true,
                ValidateAudience = true,
                ValidateLifetime = true,
                ValidateIssuerSigningKey = true,
                // Set your JWT issuer, audience, and signing key
                here
            };
        });
}
```

- **Token Generation**: Upon successful authentication, a JWT can be generated and returned to the client for subsequent requests.

2.2.3 OAuth 2.0 and OpenID Connect

OAuth 2.0 is an authorization framework that allows third-party applications to access a user's resources without sharing credentials. OpenID Connect extends OAuth 2.0 to provide identity verification.

- **Using OAuth 2.0 in .NET 6**: ASP.NET Core provides built-in support for integrating with OAuth 2.0 providers such as Google, Facebook, or Microsoft.
- **Implementing OpenID Connect**: Developers can use libraries like **IdentityServer** or built-in middleware to facilitate OpenID Connect authentication.

2.3 Authorization in .NET 6

Authorization can be implemented using role-based or policy-based approaches:

2.3.1 Role-Based Authorization

Role-based authorization assigns users to roles and grants access to resources based on those roles. This approach is straightforward and suitable for many applications.

```csharp
Copy code
[Authorize(Roles = "Admin")]
public IActionResult AdminPanel()
{
    return View();
}
```

In this example, only users assigned to the "Admin" role can access the AdminPanel action.

2.3.2 Policy-Based Authorization

Policy-based authorization provides more flexibility by allowing developers to define custom policies based on claims or other criteria.

```csharp
Copy code
services.AddAuthorization(options =>
{
    options.AddPolicy("RequireAdministratorRole", policy =>
    policy.RequireRole("Admin"));
});
```

Developers can then use the policy in controller actions:

```
csharp
Copy code
[Authorize(Policy = "RequireAdministratorRole")]
public IActionResult AdminPanel()
{
    return View();
}
```

3. Secure Coding Practices

3.1 Input Validation and Sanitization

Input validation is a critical aspect of secure coding. Developers should validate and sanitize all user inputs to prevent common vulnerabilities such as SQL injection and cross-site scripting (XSS).

3.1.1 Using Data Annotations

In ASP.NET Core, developers can use data annotations to enforce validation rules on model properties.

```
csharp
Copy code
public class UserModel
{
    [Required]
    [EmailAddress]
    public string Email { get; set; }

    [Required]
    [StringLength(100, MinimumLength = 6)]
    public string Password { get; set; }
}
```

3.1.2 Sanitizing User Inputs

When displaying user input in web applications, always sanitize the output to prevent XSS attacks. Use built-in HTML encoding methods to ensure that special characters are rendered safely.

```csharp
Copy code
@Html.Encode(userInput) // Ensure safe rendering in Razor views
```

3.2 Protecting Sensitive Data

Protecting sensitive data is essential to maintaining the confidentiality and integrity of user information.

3.2.1 Hashing Passwords

When storing user passwords, use strong hashing algorithms (e.g., PBKDF2, bcrypt, or Argon2) to hash passwords before storage.

```csharp
Copy code
using (var hasher = new PasswordHasher<User>())
{
    var hashedPassword = hasher.HashPassword(user,
    plainTextPassword);
    // Store hashedPassword in the database
}
```

3.2.2 Data Encryption

For sensitive data at rest, use encryption to protect the information. Use the **System.Security.Cryptography** namespace for implementing encryption in .NET.

```csharp
Copy code
using (var aes = Aes.Create())
{
    // Set up encryption parameters and encrypt data
```

}

3.3 Logging and Monitoring

Implement robust logging and monitoring practices to detect and respond to security incidents.

3.3.1 Logging Sensitive Actions

Log authentication attempts, authorization failures, and other critical security events. Use logging frameworks like **Serilog** or **NLog** to capture and manage logs effectively.

```csharp
Copy code
_logger.LogWarning("Unauthorized access attempt by user {UserId}",
userId);
```

3.3.2 Monitoring for Anomalies

Utilize monitoring tools to analyze logs for suspicious activities, such as repeated failed login attempts or unusual access patterns.

4. Data Protection in .NET 6

4.1 Protecting Data at Rest

When storing sensitive data, it is essential to implement measures to protect it at rest. Use encryption for databases, file systems, or any storage mechanism that holds sensitive information.

4.1.1 Using Entity Framework Core

Entity Framework Core provides built-in support for data protection, allowing developers to encrypt sensitive fields in the database.

```csharp
Copy code
protected override void OnModelCreating(ModelBuilder modelBuilder)
{
    modelBuilder.Entity<User>()
        .Property(u => u.PasswordHash)
        .HasColumnType("varchar(256)");
}
```

4.2 Protecting Data in Transit

To protect data during transmission, use secure communication protocols such as HTTPS.

4.2.1 Enforcing HTTPS

In ASP.NET Core, enforce HTTPS by configuring the middleware to redirect HTTP requests to HTTPS.

```csharp
Copy code
public void Configure(IApplicationBuilder app, IWebHostEnvironment env)
{
    app.UseHttpsRedirection();
}
```

4.3 Using ASP.NET Core Data Protection API

ASP.NET Core provides a built-in Data Protection API that simplifies the process of encrypting and decrypting data.

4.3.1 Configuring Data Protection

Configure data protection in Startup.cs to enable encryption for your application.

```csharp
Copy code
public void ConfigureServices(IServiceCollection services)
{
    services.AddDataProtection()
        .PersistKeysToFileSystem(new DirectoryInfo(@"C:\keys"));
}
```

This configuration allows the application to encrypt sensitive data and persist cryptographic keys securely.

5. Integrating Security into the Application Lifecycle

5.1 Secure Development Lifecycle (SDLC)

Integrating security practices into the application development lifecycle (SDLC) is essential for building secure applications. A Secure Development Lifecycle involves incorporating security

Chapter 12: Monitoring and Maintaining High-Performance Applications in .NET 6

B uilding high-performance applications is only part of the equation; ongoing monitoring and maintenance are crucial to ensure that performance remains optimal over time. As applications evolve and user demand fluctuates, it is essential to have strategies in place for monitoring application health, diagnosing performance issues, and maintaining code quality. This chapter will explore the various approaches and tools for monitoring and maintaining high-performance applications built with .NET 6, emphasizing the importance of proactive performance management.

1. Importance of Monitoring in High-Performance Applications

1.1 The Need for Monitoring

Monitoring is the continuous observation of an application's performance and health to ensure it operates efficiently and reliably. In high-performance applications, monitoring is vital for several reasons:

- **Real-Time Insights**: Monitoring provides real-time visibility into application performance, enabling teams to identify and address issues as they arise.

- **User Experience**: Performance issues can lead to degraded user experiences. Monitoring helps detect bottlenecks and other problems before they impact users.
- **Capacity Planning**: Monitoring data can inform capacity planning decisions, ensuring that the application can handle increased loads or growth.

1.2 Key Metrics to Monitor

When monitoring high-performance applications, several key metrics should be tracked:

- **Response Time**: Measure how long it takes for the application to respond to user requests.
- **Throughput**: Track the number of requests processed per unit of time to gauge overall application performance.
- **Error Rates**: Monitor the frequency of errors (e.g., HTTP 500 errors) to identify potential issues with application reliability.
- **Resource Utilization**: Keep an eye on CPU, memory, disk I/O, and network usage to ensure efficient resource utilization.
- **Garbage Collection Metrics**: Track garbage collection (GC) frequency and duration to identify potential memory management issues.

2. Monitoring Tools and Techniques in .NET 6

2.1 Application Insights

Azure Application Insights is a powerful application performance management (APM) service that provides monitoring and analytics capabilities for .NET applications.

2.1.1 Setting Up Application Insights

To integrate Application Insights into a .NET 6 application:

1. **Add Application Insights SDK**: Install the Application Insights SDK via NuGet.

```bash
Copy code
dotnet add package Microsoft.ApplicationInsights.AspNetCore
```

1. **Configure Application Insights**: Add the Application Insights service in the Startup.cs file.

```csharp
Copy code
public void ConfigureServices(IServiceCollection services)
{
    services.AddApplicationInsightsTelemetry();
}
```

1. **Instrument Code**: Use the Application Insights API to log custom events, exceptions, and metrics.

```csharp
Copy code
var telemetryClient = new TelemetryClient();
telemetryClient.TrackEvent("MyCustomEvent");
```

2.1.2 Features of Application Insights

- **Performance Monitoring**: Track response times, request rates, and failure rates to gain insights into application performance.
- **Dependency Tracking**: Monitor external dependencies (e.g., databases,

APIs) to identify potential bottlenecks.

- **Exception Tracking**: Automatically capture unhandled exceptions and track them for analysis.
- **Live Metrics Stream**: View real-time performance metrics to diagnose issues as they occur.

2.2 Azure Monitor

Azure Monitor provides a comprehensive solution for monitoring Azure applications and resources. It integrates with Application Insights and offers additional capabilities for monitoring infrastructure and services.

2.2.1 Key Features of Azure Monitor

- **Log Analytics**: Analyze logs and metrics from various sources using Kusto Query Language (KQL).
- **Alerts and Notifications**: Set up alerts to notify the team when certain thresholds or conditions are met, enabling proactive responses to performance issues.
- **Workbooks**: Create custom dashboards and reports to visualize performance metrics and trends.

2.3 OpenTelemetry

OpenTelemetry is an open-source observability framework that provides a standardized way to collect metrics, traces, and logs from applications.

2.3.1 Integrating OpenTelemetry in .NET 6

To implement OpenTelemetry in a .NET 6 application:

1. **Add OpenTelemetry NuGet Packages**:

```bash
Copy code
dotnet add package OpenTelemetry
dotnet add package OpenTelemetry.Extensions.Hosting
```

1. **Configure OpenTelemetry**:

```csharp
Copy code
public void ConfigureServices(IServiceCollection services)
{
    services.AddOpenTelemetryTracing(builder =>
    {
        builder
            .AddAspNetCoreInstrumentation()
            .AddHttpClientInstrumentation()
            .SetResourceBuilder(ResourceBuilder.
CreateDefault().AddService("MyServiceName"));
    });
}
```

1. **Exporting Data**: Configure the exporter to send collected telemetry data to a monitoring backend (e.g., Jaeger, Prometheus, Azure Monitor).

2.4 Logging Frameworks

Effective logging is essential for diagnosing issues and understanding application behavior. Several logging frameworks are commonly used in .NET applications:

2.4.1 Serilog

Serilog is a popular structured logging library for .NET that provides powerful features for logging events and metrics.

- **Structured Logging**: Serilog allows developers to log structured data, enabling richer queries and insights.

```csharp
Copy code
Log.Information("User {UserId} logged in at {LoginTime}", userId,
DateTime.UtcNow);
```

- **Sink Configuration**: Serilog supports various sinks (outputs) for logging data, including files, databases, and cloud services.

2.4.2 NLog

NLog is another flexible logging framework that supports a wide range of logging targets and configurations.

- **Configuration Flexibility**: NLog allows developers to configure logging targets and layouts through XML or code.
- **Asynchronous Logging**: NLog supports asynchronous logging to improve performance and reduce logging overhead on application responsiveness.

3. Diagnosing Performance Issues

3.1 Identifying Bottlenecks

Monitoring tools provide valuable insights into application performance, allowing developers to identify bottlenecks. Common areas to investigate include:

- **Slow Requests**: Analyze response times for different endpoints and identify slow-performing requests.
- **High Error Rates**: Investigate any spikes in error rates, particularly

500-series errors, which indicate server issues.

- **Resource Utilization**: Monitor CPU and memory usage to identify components that are consuming excessive resources.

3.2 Profiling Applications

Profiling tools can help diagnose performance issues by providing detailed insights into application behavior:

3.2.1 Visual Studio Diagnostic Tools

Visual Studio includes built-in diagnostic tools that enable developers to profile CPU and memory usage:

- **CPU Usage**: Analyze CPU consumption to identify methods or operations that are consuming excessive processing power.
- **Memory Usage**: Track memory allocations to identify potential memory leaks or excessive garbage collection activity.

3.2.2 dotTrace

dotTrace is a performance profiling tool from JetBrains that provides in-depth insights into application performance.

- **CPU Profiling**: Analyze method execution time to identify hotspots in the application.
- **Memory Profiling**: Track memory allocations and object lifetimes to identify potential leaks or inefficiencies.

3.3 Conducting Root Cause Analysis

When performance issues arise, it is essential to conduct a root cause analysis (RCA) to identify the underlying causes. RCA involves examining logs, monitoring data, and profiling results to pinpoint the source of the problem.

- **Review Logs**: Analyze application logs for any unusual patterns or errors that may indicate underlying issues.

- **Correlate Metrics**: Look for correlations between different performance metrics (e.g., increased response times and high CPU usage) to identify potential bottlenecks.

4. Maintaining Application Performance

4.1 Regular Performance Audits

Conducting regular performance audits helps ensure that applications maintain optimal performance over time. Audits should include:

- **Load Testing**: Regularly perform load tests to validate that the application can handle expected traffic levels.
- **Code Reviews**: Conduct code reviews with a focus on performance to identify potential inefficiencies or anti-patterns.

4.2 Refactoring and Optimization

As applications evolve, developers may need to refactor and optimize code to maintain performance:

4.2.1 Continuous Improvement

Implement a culture of continuous improvement, encouraging developers to identify areas for optimization and to adopt best practices.

4.2.2 Code Optimization Techniques

Optimize critical code paths by applying techniques such as:

- **Inlining Methods**: For small, frequently called methods, consider inlining to reduce method call overhead.
- **Reducing Memory Allocations**: Use object pooling and value types to minimize memory allocations and garbage collection pressure.

4.3 Keeping Dependencies Up-to-Date

Regularly updating application dependencies is essential for maintaining performance and security. Newer versions of libraries and frameworks often include performance improvements and bug fixes.

- **Dependency Management**: Use tools like NuGet Package Manager to manage and update dependencies efficiently.

4.4 Training and Knowledge Sharing

Investing in training and knowledge sharing among team members helps ensure that all developers are aware of performance best practices and new tools.

- **Internal Workshops**: Conduct workshops and training sessions to share insights on performance optimization techniques.
- **Documentation**: Maintain up-to-date documentation on performance guidelines and best practices for the development team.

5. Scaling for Future Growth

5.1 Planning for Scalability

As applications grow, proactive planning for scalability is essential. Consider the following strategies:

5.1.1 Load Balancing

Implement load balancing to distribute incoming requests across multiple instances of the application. This helps prevent any single instance from becoming a bottleneck.

- **Application Gateway**: Use an application gateway or load balancer to route traffic efficiently to multiple instances.

5.1.2 Auto-Scaling

In cloud environments, consider implementing auto-scaling to automatically adjust the number of running instances based on traffic patterns.

- **Azure App Service Auto-Scaling**: Configure Azure App Service to automatically scale out or in based on defined rules and metrics.

5.2 Planning for Data Growth

As data volumes increase, it's important to have a strategy for managing and scaling data storage:

5.2.1 Database Scaling

Evaluate database scaling options, including:

- **Sharding**: Distributing data across multiple databases or instances to reduce contention and improve performance.
- **Read Replicas**: Using read replicas to offload read operations from the primary database.

5.2.2 Data Retention Policies

Implement data retention policies to manage data growth and ensure that old data is archived or deleted according to business requirements.

5.3 Continuous Deployment and Integration

Adopt continuous deployment and integration practices to ensure that new features and optimizations are delivered quickly and reliably:

5.3.1 CI/CD Pipelines

Implement CI/CD pipelines that automate the build, test, and deployment processes. This helps catch performance regressions early and allows for rapid iteration.

- **Automated Performance Tests**: Include performance tests in the

CI/CD pipeline to ensure that changes do not degrade application performance.

5.3.2 Staging Environments

Use staging environments to test performance optimizations and new features in a controlled setting before deploying them to production.

6. Conclusion

Monitoring and maintaining high-performance applications in .NET 6 is a continuous process that requires a proactive approach. By leveraging monitoring tools, diagnosing performance issues, and implementing best practices for maintenance, developers can ensure that applications remain performant and responsive over time.

This chapter explored various strategies for monitoring application performance, including the use of Application Insights, Azure Monitor, and OpenTelemetry. We also discussed the importance of logging, diagnosing performance issues, and the necessity of regular performance audits. Maintaining application performance involves ongoing optimization, keeping dependencies up to date, and fostering a culture of continuous improvement.

As applications evolve and user demands change, effective monitoring and maintenance will be essential for achieving long-term success in high-performance application development. By prioritizing performance management, developers can create systems that not only meet current requirements but also adapt to future growth, ensuring a positive user experience and sustained application reliability.

Chapter 13: Leveraging Cloud Services for Scalability and Performance in .NET 6 Applications

As organizations strive to build scalable and high-performance applications, cloud computing has become a key enabler of modern software development. Cloud services offer a wide range of tools and infrastructure that allow developers to focus on building applications while abstracting away many operational concerns. This chapter will explore how to leverage cloud services to enhance the scalability and performance of applications built with .NET 6. We will discuss various cloud providers, architectures, and strategies to maximize the benefits of cloud computing.

1. Understanding Cloud Computing

1.1 What is Cloud Computing?

Cloud computing refers to the delivery of computing resources—such as servers, storage, databases, networking, software, and analytics—over the internet ("the cloud"). It allows organizations to access and utilize resources on-demand without the need to own and manage physical infrastructure.

1.2 Key Characteristics of Cloud Computing

Cloud computing has several defining characteristics:

- **On-Demand Self-Service**: Users can provision computing resources automatically without requiring human intervention from the service provider.
- **Broad Network Access**: Cloud services are accessible over the internet from a variety of devices, including desktops, laptops, tablets, and smartphones.
- **Resource Pooling**: Resources are pooled to serve multiple customers using a multi-tenant model, with physical and virtual resources dynamically assigned and reassigned according to demand.
- **Rapid Elasticity**: Resources can be scaled up or down quickly based on demand, allowing for flexibility in handling varying workloads.
- **Measured Service**: Resource usage can be monitored, controlled, and reported, providing transparency for both the provider and the customer.

1.3 Benefits of Cloud Computing for Scalability and Performance

Leveraging cloud computing for application development offers several advantages:

- **Scalability**: Cloud services enable applications to scale horizontally by adding or removing resources as needed, accommodating spikes in demand.
- **Performance Optimization**: Cloud providers offer managed services that are optimized for performance, including databases, caching solutions, and content delivery networks (CDNs).
- **Cost Efficiency**: Organizations can reduce infrastructure costs by paying only for the resources they use, allowing for better budget management.
- **Rapid Development and Deployment**: Cloud services enable faster

161

development and deployment cycles, allowing organizations to respond quickly to market demands.

2. Cloud Providers and Services

2.1 Major Cloud Providers

Several major cloud providers offer a comprehensive range of services for application development, including:

- **Microsoft Azure**: Azure is a cloud computing platform that provides a variety of services, including computing, storage, databases, networking, and analytics. It integrates seamlessly with .NET applications.
- **Amazon Web Services (AWS)**: AWS is a comprehensive cloud platform that offers a wide range of services, including computing power (EC2), storage (S3), and database management (RDS).
- **Google Cloud Platform (GCP)**: GCP offers a suite of cloud services, including computing (Google Compute Engine), storage (Google Cloud Storage), and machine learning capabilities.

2.2 Choosing the Right Cloud Provider

When selecting a cloud provider, consider factors such as:

- **Service Availability**: Ensure that the provider offers the specific services needed for your application.
- **Pricing Model**: Evaluate the pricing structure to determine the cost-effectiveness of the services.
- **Integration with Existing Tools**: Consider how well the cloud provider integrates with existing development tools and workflows.
- **Global Reach**: Assess the provider's data center locations and network capabilities to ensure low latency for users worldwide.

3. Architecting Scalable Applications on the Cloud

3.1 Microservices Architecture

Microservices architecture is an effective approach for building scalable applications in the cloud. It involves breaking down applications into smaller, independent services that can be developed, deployed, and scaled independently.

3.1.1 Advantages of Microservices in the Cloud

- **Independent Scaling**: Each microservice can be scaled independently based on its specific load and performance requirements.
- **Fault Isolation**: The failure of one microservice does not affect the entire application, improving overall resilience.
- **Technology Diversity**: Different microservices can use different technologies and languages, allowing teams to choose the best tools for their needs.

3.2 Serverless Architecture

Serverless architecture abstracts infrastructure management, allowing developers to focus on writing code while the cloud provider handles scaling and resource allocation.

3.2.1 Benefits of Serverless Architecture

- **Automatic Scaling**: Serverless functions automatically scale in response to demand, ensuring optimal resource utilization.
- **Reduced Operational Overhead**: Developers do not need to manage servers or worry about infrastructure provisioning.
- **Event-Driven Processing**: Serverless architectures are well-suited for event-driven applications, where functions are triggered by events such as HTTP requests, timers, or database changes.

3.3 Event-Driven Architecture

Event-driven architecture (EDA) is a design pattern that uses events to trigger actions and communications between services. This approach can enhance scalability by decoupling components and allowing for asynchronous processing.

3.3.1 Benefits of Event-Driven Architecture

- **Loose Coupling**: Services communicate through events, reducing dependencies and allowing for independent evolution.
- **Scalability**: Event-driven systems can handle high volumes of events without blocking or impacting performance.
- **Real-Time Processing**: EDA enables real-time processing of events, making it suitable for applications requiring immediate responses.

4. Cloud Services for Scalability and Performance

4.1 Compute Services

Cloud providers offer various compute services to support scalable application architectures:

4.1.1 Virtual Machines (VMs)

VMs allow developers to create scalable compute instances in the cloud. Providers such as Azure, AWS, and GCP offer a range of VM types optimized for different workloads.

- **Auto-Scaling**: Configure auto-scaling policies to automatically adjust the number of VM instances based on demand.

4.1.2 Container Services

Containers provide a lightweight and portable way to package applications. Cloud providers offer managed container services for deploying and scaling containerized applications.

- **Azure Kubernetes Service (AKS)**: A managed Kubernetes service that simplifies the deployment and management of containerized applications.
- **Amazon Elastic Kubernetes Service (EKS)**: A fully managed Kubernetes service that allows users to run Kubernetes clusters on AWS.

4.1.3 Serverless Functions

Serverless functions, such as Azure Functions and AWS Lambda, allow developers to run code without managing servers. These functions automatically scale based on incoming requests.

- **Event Triggers**: Functions can be triggered by various events, including HTTP requests, database changes, or messages from a queue.

4.2 Storage Services

Effective data management is essential for high-performance applications. Cloud providers offer various storage solutions to support scalability and performance.

4.2.1 Blob Storage

Blob storage is designed for storing large amounts of unstructured data, such as images, videos, and backups. It provides scalability and high availability.

- **Azure Blob Storage**: Offers tiered storage options for different access patterns, including hot, cool, and archive tiers.
- **Amazon S3**: A scalable object storage service that provides durability and low-latency access to data.

4.2.2 Managed Databases

Managed database services abstract the complexities of database management while providing scalability and performance.

- **Azure SQL Database**: A fully managed relational database service that offers scaling options, including elastic pools and serverless tiers.
- **Amazon RDS**: A managed relational database service that supports various database engines, including MySQL, PostgreSQL, and SQL Server.

4.3 Caching Services

Caching is critical for enhancing application performance by reducing latency and offloading database queries.

4.3.1 In-Memory Caching

In-memory caching solutions store frequently accessed data in memory for quick retrieval.

- **Azure Cache for Redis**: A managed Redis cache service that provides fast data access and supports pub/sub messaging patterns.
- **Amazon ElastiCache**: A managed service for Redis and Memcached that enables scalable in-memory caching.

4.3.2 Content Delivery Networks (CDNs)

CDNs cache and deliver content from locations closer to users, reducing latency and improving load times.

- **Azure CDN**: A global CDN service that accelerates the delivery of web content.
- **Amazon CloudFront**: A fast and secure CDN service that integrates with other AWS services.

4.4 Monitoring and Analytics Services

Monitoring and analytics are essential for maintaining the performance and health of cloud applications.

4.4.1 Application Insights

As discussed earlier, Application Insights provides comprehensive monitoring for .NET applications. It helps track performance metrics, exceptions, and user interactions.

4.4.2 Azure Monitor

Azure Monitor collects and analyzes performance data across Azure resources, providing insights into application health and resource utilization.

4.4.3 Logging and Analytics Tools

Utilize logging and analytics tools such as Azure Log Analytics and Amazon CloudWatch to collect, analyze, and visualize log data.

5. Implementing Scalability in .NET 6 Applications

5.1 Application Design Patterns

When building scalable applications with .NET 6, certain design patterns can facilitate scalability and performance:

5.1.1 Repository Pattern

The repository pattern abstracts data access logic, making it easier to manage data interactions and switch between different data sources or storage mechanisms.

```csharp
Copy code
public interface IRepository<T>
{
    Task<T> GetByIdAsync(int id);
    Task<IEnumerable<T>> GetAllAsync();
    Task AddAsync(T entity);
    Task UpdateAsync(T entity);
    Task DeleteAsync(int id);
}
```

5.1.2 Unit of Work Pattern

The unit of work pattern allows developers to group multiple operations into a single transaction, ensuring data consistency and reducing the number of database calls.

```csharp
Copy code
public interface IUnitOfWork : IDisposable
{
    IRepository<T> Repository<T>() where T : class;
    Task<int> SaveChangesAsync();
}
```

5.2 Configuration and Deployment Best Practices

Proper configuration and deployment practices can enhance the performance and scalability of .NET applications:

5.2.1 Environment-Specific Configurations

Use configuration settings to manage environment-specific settings, such as connection strings and API keys. ASP.NET Core supports various configuration sources, including JSON files, environment variables, and Azure Key Vault.

```csharp
Copy code
public void ConfigureServices(IServiceCollection services)
{
    services.Configure<
DatabaseSettings>
(Configuration.
GetSection("Database"));
}
```

5.2.2 Containerization

Containerize .NET applications using Docker to ensure consistent deployments across different environments. Define a Dockerfile that specifies the build and runtime environment for the application.

```
dockerfile
Copy code
# Use the official .NET SDK image for building the application
FROM mcr.microsoft.
com/dotnet/sdk:6.0 AS build
WORKDIR /src
COPY ["MyApp/MyApp.csproj", "MyApp/"]
RUN dotnet restore "MyApp/MyApp.csproj"
COPY . .
WORKDIR "/src/MyApp"
RUN dotnet build "MyApp.csproj" -c Release -o /app/build

# Use the official .NET runtime image
for running the application
FROM mcr.microsoft.com/dotnet/aspnet:6.0 AS runtime
WORKDIR /app
COPY --from=build /app/build .
ENTRYPOINT ["dotnet", "MyApp.dll"]
```

5.3 Continuous Integration and Continuous Deployment (CI/CD)

Implement CI/CD pipelines to automate the build, test, and deployment processes. This ensures that changes can be rapidly delivered while maintaining quality and performance.

5.3.1 Azure DevOps

Azure DevOps provides a robust platform for implementing CI/CD pipelines for .NET applications.

- **Build Pipelines**: Configure build pipelines to automatically build and test the application upon code changes.
- **Release Pipelines**: Use release pipelines to deploy the application to various environments (e.g., staging, production) with automated approvals and monitoring.

5.3.2 GitHub Actions

GitHub Actions offers a powerful automation framework for CI/CD directly within GitHub repositories.

- **Workflows**: Define workflows to build, test, and deploy applications based on triggers such as pull requests or merges.

6. Conclusion

Leveraging cloud services is a powerful strategy for building scalable and high-performance applications with .NET 6. Cloud computing provides the flexibility, resources, and tools necessary to meet the demands of modern application development. By understanding cloud computing principles, utilizing cloud services effectively, and implementing best practices for scalability and performance, developers can create robust applications that are prepared for future growth.

This chapter covered various cloud providers, architectures, and services that enhance scalability and performance. We explored key concepts such as microservices, serverless architecture, event-driven architecture, and the various services available for compute, storage, caching, and monitoring. Additionally, we discussed design patterns, configuration best practices, and the importance of CI/CD in maintaining application performance.

As technology continues to evolve, organizations must adapt their approaches to building and deploying applications. By leveraging the power of cloud computing and .NET 6, developers can create scalable, high-performance applications that deliver exceptional user experiences and meet the challenges of tomorrow's digital landscape.

Chapter 14: Ensuring Data Security and Compliance in .NET 6 Applications

In today's digital landscape, data security and compliance have become paramount concerns for software developers and organizations. As applications increasingly handle sensitive information, ensuring that data is protected from unauthorized access, breaches, and other threats is crucial. Additionally, many industries are subject to regulations that mandate specific data handling and privacy practices. This chapter will explore the importance of data security and compliance in .NET 6 applications, covering best practices, security frameworks, and strategies to safeguard sensitive data while adhering to legal requirements.

1. Understanding Data Security

1.1 What is Data Security?

Data security encompasses the processes and measures taken to protect digital data from unauthorized access, corruption, or theft throughout its lifecycle. It involves implementing technical controls, policies, and procedures to ensure that data remains confidential, integral, and available to authorized users.

1.2 Importance of Data Security

The significance of data security cannot be overstated, particularly in light of increasing cyber threats and data breaches. Key reasons for prioritizing data security include:

- **Protection of Sensitive Information**: Organizations handle various types of sensitive data, including personal identifiable information (PII), financial records, and healthcare data. Protecting this information is vital to maintain user trust and comply with regulations.
- **Compliance with Regulations**: Many industries are subject to strict regulations governing data protection (e.g., GDPR, HIPAA). Non-compliance can result in significant penalties and legal ramifications.
- **Preventing Financial Loss**: Data breaches can lead to substantial financial losses, both from direct costs (e.g., fines, legal fees) and indirect costs (e.g., reputational damage, loss of customers).
- **Mitigating Risks**: Implementing data security measures helps reduce the risk of cyberattacks, ensuring business continuity and protecting organizational assets.

2. Compliance Regulations

2.1 Overview of Compliance Regulations

Compliance regulations are legal frameworks that dictate how organizations must handle and protect data. Some of the most common regulations include:

- **General Data Protection Regulation (GDPR)**: A comprehensive data protection regulation in the European Union that governs the processing of personal data and emphasizes user consent, data access rights, and breach notification requirements.
- **Health Insurance Portability and Accountability Act (HIPAA)**: A U.S. regulation that sets standards for protecting sensitive patient information

in the healthcare industry.

- **Payment Card Industry Data Security Standard (PCI DSS)**: A set of security standards designed to protect card information during transactions and storage.
- **California Consumer Privacy Act (CCPA)**: A state law that enhances privacy rights and consumer protection for residents of California, including rights related to data access, deletion, and sales.

2.2 Implications of Compliance Regulations

Organizations must understand the implications of compliance regulations when developing applications. Non-compliance can lead to:

- **Financial Penalties**: Regulatory bodies can impose fines for non-compliance, which can range from thousands to millions of dollars depending on the severity of the violation.
- **Legal Consequences**: Organizations may face lawsuits from consumers or stakeholders for mishandling sensitive data.
- **Reputational Damage**: A data breach or failure to comply can lead to a loss of trust from customers, affecting business relationships and sales.

3. Data Protection Strategies in .NET 6

3.1 Secure Coding Practices

Adopting secure coding practices is essential for developing secure applications. In .NET 6, developers should implement the following strategies:

3.1.1 Input Validation and Sanitization

All user inputs should be validated and sanitized to prevent common vulnerabilities such as SQL injection and cross-site scripting (XSS).

- **Use Data Annotations**: Implement data annotations in models to enforce validation rules.

```csharp
Copy code
public class UserModel
{
    [Required]
    [EmailAddress]
    public string Email { get; set; }

    [Required]
    [StringLength(100, MinimumLength = 6)]
    public string Password { get; set; }
}
```

- **Sanitize Outputs**: When displaying user input, ensure that outputs are sanitized to prevent XSS attacks.

```csharp
Copy code
@Html.Encode(userInput) // Ensure safe rendering in Razor views
```

3.1.2 Principle of Least Privilege

Apply the principle of least privilege by granting users and components the minimum permissions necessary to perform their tasks. This reduces the risk of unauthorized access and limits the potential impact of a breach.

3.2 Data Encryption

Encryption is a critical component of data security, ensuring that sensitive information remains confidential.

3.2.1 Encrypting Data at Rest

Data at rest refers to data stored on disk or in databases. Encrypting this data helps protect it from unauthorized access.

- **Using Entity Framework Core**: When using Entity Framework Core, consider implementing encryption for sensitive fields before storing them in the database.

```csharp
Copy code
public class User
{
    public int Id { get; set; }

    [Encrypted] // Custom attribute to indicate encryption
    public string PasswordHash { get; set; }
}
```

3.2.2 Encrypting Data in Transit

Data in transit refers to data being transmitted over networks. Using secure communication protocols such as HTTPS ensures that data is encrypted during transmission.

- **Enforcing HTTPS**: Configure your ASP.NET Core application to enforce HTTPS by redirecting HTTP requests.

```csharp
Copy code
public void Configure(IApplicationBuilder app, IWebHostEnvironment env)
{
    app.UseHttpsRedirection();
}
```

3.3 Authentication and Authorization

Implementing strong authentication and authorization mechanisms is essential for protecting sensitive data.

3.3.1 ASP.NET Core Identity

ASP.NET Core Identity provides a robust framework for managing user accounts, authentication, and authorization. It includes features such as:

- **User Registration and Management**: Allow users to create accounts, manage passwords, and reset forgotten passwords.
- **Claims-Based Authentication**: Assign claims to users that represent their permissions and roles within the application.

3.3.2 Role-Based and Policy-Based Authorization

Implement both role-based and policy-based authorization to control access to resources effectively.

- **Role-Based Authorization**: Use role-based authorization to restrict access based on user roles.

```csharp
Copy code
[Authorize(Roles = "Admin")]
public IActionResult AdminPanel()
{
    return View();
}
```

- **Policy-Based Authorization**: Create custom policies for more granular control over access.

```csharp
Copy code
services.AddAuthorization(options =>
{
    options.AddPolicy("RequireAdministratorRole", policy =>
    policy.RequireRole("Admin"));
});
```

4. Data Handling and Storage Practices

4.1 Data Retention Policies

Establishing data retention policies helps ensure that sensitive data is retained only as long as necessary for business or legal purposes. This practice also helps minimize the risk of data breaches.

4.1.1 Define Retention Periods

Define clear retention periods for different types of data based on regulatory requirements and business needs. Regularly review and update these policies as necessary.

4.1.2 Implement Data Deletion Procedures

Implement procedures for securely deleting data that is no longer needed. This includes:

- **Secure Deletion Methods**: Use secure deletion methods that ensure data cannot be recovered after it is deleted.
- **Automated Deletion**: Automate the deletion process based on defined retention policies to minimize the risk of human error.

4.2 Data Backup and Recovery

Implementing a robust data backup and recovery strategy is essential for protecting against data loss due to accidents, corruption, or attacks.

4.2.1 Regular Backups

Schedule regular backups of databases and critical data. Use automated tools to ensure consistency and minimize downtime.

4.2.2 Test Recovery Procedures

Regularly test data recovery procedures to ensure that data can be restored quickly and accurately in the event of a failure.

5. Security Frameworks and Tools

5.1 .NET Security Features

.NET 6 provides a range of built-in security features and libraries that can help developers implement secure applications.

5.1.1 Data Protection API

The Data Protection API in .NET provides a simple way to protect sensitive data, such as connection strings, keys, and passwords.

```csharp
Copy code
public void ConfigureServices(IServiceCollection services)
{
    services.AddDataProtection()
        .PersistKeysToFileSystem(new DirectoryInfo(@"C:\keys"))
        .SetApplicationName("MyApp");
}
```

5.1.2 Secure Sockets Layer (SSL) and Transport Layer Security (TLS)

Utilize SSL/TLS to secure communications between clients and servers. Ensure that your application is configured to use the latest security protocols.

5.2 Third-Party Security Tools

Consider integrating third-party security tools to enhance your application's security posture.

5.2.1 Web Application Firewalls (WAF)

Web application firewalls provide an additional layer of security by filtering and monitoring HTTP traffic between a web application and the internet. They help protect against common web vulnerabilities such as SQL injection and XSS.

5.2.2 Security Information and Event Management (SIEM)

SIEM tools aggregate and analyze security event data from across the organization, providing insights into potential threats and vulnerabilities. This allows for timely detection and response to security incidents.

6. Continuous Security Practices

6.1 Security Testing and Vulnerability Assessment

Regular security testing is essential for identifying and addressing vulnerabilities in applications.

6.1.1 Static Application Security Testing (SAST)

SAST tools analyze source code for vulnerabilities without executing the application. Incorporate SAST tools into the development process to catch security issues early.

6.1.2 Dynamic Application Security Testing (DAST)

DAST tools test running applications for vulnerabilities by simulating attacks. Perform DAST as part of the testing phase before deployment.

6.2 Secure DevOps Practices

Integrating security into the DevOps process (DevSecOps) ensures that security is a fundamental part of the development lifecycle.

6.2.1 Automated Security Scans

Implement automated security scans in the CI/CD pipeline to catch vulnerabilities before code is merged or deployed.

6.2.2 Security Training for Developers

Provide regular security training and awareness programs for developers to keep them informed about best practices and emerging threats.

6.3 Incident Response Plan

Establish a comprehensive incident response plan to address security incidents effectively. Key components include:

- **Preparation**: Define roles and responsibilities, and ensure team members are trained.
- **Detection**: Implement monitoring and alerting to detect security incidents.
- **Containment**: Establish procedures for containing security breaches to minimize impact.
- **Eradication and Recovery**: Define steps for eradicating threats and recovering systems after an incident.
- **Post-Incident Review**: Conduct a post-incident review to analyze what happened and improve future response efforts.

7. Conclusion

Ensuring data security and compliance in .NET 6 applications is a multi-faceted challenge that requires a comprehensive approach. By implementing robust security measures, adhering to compliance regulations, and leveraging the security features provided by .NET 6, developers can create applications that protect sensitive data and maintain user trust.

This chapter explored various aspects of data security, including secure coding practices, authentication and authorization mechanisms, data encryption, and effective data handling strategies. We also discussed security frameworks, third-party tools, and the importance of continuous security practices.

As the digital landscape continues to evolve and new threats emerge, organizations must remain vigilant in their approach to data security and compliance. By prioritizing security throughout the application lifecycle and integrating security into the development process, developers can build resilient applications that not only perform well but also protect sensitive information from unauthorized access and breaches.

In conclusion, embracing a culture of security and compliance will enable organizations to navigate the complexities of data protection while ensuring that their applications continue to deliver value and meet the needs of users in an increasingly challenging environment.

Chapter 15: Best Practices for Deploying High-Performance Applications in .NET 6

As organizations strive to deliver high-performance applications, effective deployment practices become crucial. Deployment is the process of delivering the application to end-users, and it significantly impacts application performance, reliability, and user experience. This chapter will cover best practices for deploying high-performance applications built with .NET 6, including strategies for continuous deployment, monitoring performance post-deployment, managing configurations, and ensuring rollback capabilities.

1. Understanding Deployment Strategies

1.1 What is Application Deployment?

Application deployment involves the processes and activities required to make an application available for use. This includes packaging the application, transferring it to the production environment, configuring the environment, and enabling access for end-users.

1.2 The Importance of Deployment Practices

Effective deployment practices are essential for several reasons:

- **User Experience**: Smooth deployments minimize downtime and disruptions for users, enhancing their experience.
- **Performance Optimization**: Well-planned deployments ensure that applications perform optimally in the production environment.
- **Risk Mitigation**: Implementing best practices reduces the risk of deployment failures and allows for quick recovery when issues arise.

1.3 Common Deployment Models

Different deployment models are available, each with its advantages and use cases:

- **Manual Deployment**: Involves manually transferring files to the production server. This model can be error-prone and is generally discouraged for complex applications.
- **Automated Deployment**: Uses scripts or tools to automate the deployment process, reducing human error and increasing efficiency.
- **Continuous Deployment**: Automatically deploys code changes to production as soon as they pass testing, enabling rapid delivery of new features and updates.

2. Preparing for Deployment

2.1 Application Packaging

Proper application packaging is the first step in the deployment process. In .NET 6, applications can be packaged using various methods:

2.1.1 Publish Command

The dotnet publish command is used to compile the application and prepare it for deployment. This command creates a directory containing the necessary files, including the application binaries and dependencies.

```bash
Copy code
dotnet publish -c Release -o ./publish
```

This command builds the application in release mode and outputs the published files to the ./publish directory.

2.1.2 Docker Containers

Containerization provides a consistent environment for applications, simplifying deployment across different environments. Create a Dockerfile to define the application's container image.

```dockerfile
Copy code
# Use the official .NET SDK image for building the application
FROM mcr.microsoft.com/dotnet/sdk:6.0 AS build
WORKDIR /src
COPY ["MyApp/MyApp.csproj", "MyApp/"]
RUN dotnet restore "MyApp/MyApp.csproj"
COPY . .
WORKDIR "/src/MyApp"
RUN dotnet build "MyApp.csproj" -c Release -o /app/build

# Use the official .NET runtime image for running the application
FROM mcr.microsoft.com/dotnet/aspnet:6.0 AS runtime
WORKDIR /app
COPY --from=build /app/build .
ENTRYPOINT ["dotnet", "MyApp.dll"]
```

2.2 Environment Configuration

Configuration management is critical for ensuring that applications behave as expected in different environments (development, staging, production). Utilize configuration files, environment variables, and secrets management to manage settings.

2.2.1 Configuration Files

.NET 6 applications typically use appsettings.json files for configuration. Use separate files for different environments (e.g., appsettings.Development.json, appsettings.Production.json) to manage environment-specific settings.

```json
Copy code
{
  "ConnectionStrings": {
    "DefaultConnection": "Server=prod-server;Database=mydb;User
    Id=myuser;Password=mypassword;"
  },
  "Logging": {
    "LogLevel": {
      "Default": "Information",
      "Microsoft": "Warning"
    }
  }
}
```

2.2.2 Environment Variables

Use environment variables to override configuration settings at runtime, particularly sensitive information like connection strings and API keys.

```bash
Copy code
setx ConnectionStrings__DefaultConnection
"Server=prod-server;Database=mydb;User
Id=myuser;Password=mypassword;"
```

2.3 CI/CD Pipeline Setup

Implementing a CI/CD (Continuous Integration/Continuous Deployment) pipeline automates the build, test, and deployment processes, ensuring a smooth and consistent deployment experience.

2.3.1 Azure DevOps Pipelines

Azure DevOps provides robust support for building CI/CD pipelines for .NET applications.

- **Build Pipeline**: Automate the build process to compile the application and run tests.
- **Release Pipeline**: Set up release pipelines to deploy the application to different environments (staging, production) with automated approvals.

2.3.2 GitHub Actions

GitHub Actions allows developers to create workflows for CI/CD directly within their GitHub repositories.

```yaml
Copy code
name: .NET 6 CI

on:
  push:
    branches: [ main ]

jobs:
  build:
    runs-on: ubuntu-latest
    steps:
      - uses: actions/checkout@v2
      - name: Setup .NET
        uses: actions/setup-dotnet@v1
        with:
          dotnet-version: '6.0.x'
      - name: Install dependencies
```

```
    run: dotnet restore
- name: Build
    run: dotnet build --configuration Release --no-restore
- name: Test
    run: dotnet test --no-restore --verbosity normal
```

3. Deployment Strategies

3.1 Blue-Green Deployment

Blue-green deployment is a strategy that reduces downtime and risk by maintaining two identical environments, "blue" and "green." The new version of the application is deployed to the inactive environment (e.g., "green"), and once validated, traffic is switched from the active environment (e.g., "blue") to the new one.

3.1.1 Benefits of Blue-Green Deployment

- **Zero Downtime**: Switching traffic between environments minimizes downtime for users.
- **Rollback Capability**: If issues are detected, it's easy to revert traffic back to the previous environment.
- **Easy Testing**: The new version can be tested in production conditions before full deployment.

3.2 Rolling Deployment

In a rolling deployment, the application is updated in increments, with a subset of instances receiving the new version at a time. This approach helps ensure that not all instances are updated simultaneously.

3.2.1 Benefits of Rolling Deployment

- **Gradual Rollout**: Allows for gradual exposure of new features, reducing risk.

- **Monitoring During Deployment**: Performance can be monitored during the rollout, allowing for adjustments if issues arise.
- **Minimal Impact**: The impact of a failure is limited to a small number of instances.

3.3 Canary Deployment

Canary deployment involves releasing the new version of an application to a small subset of users before rolling it out to the entire user base. This approach allows developers to validate the new version under real user conditions.

3.3.1 Benefits of Canary Deployment

- **Risk Mitigation**: Issues can be identified and resolved with minimal impact on users.
- **User Feedback**: Collect user feedback on new features before a full rollout.
- **A/B Testing**: Use canary deployments for A/B testing to compare the performance of the new version against the existing version.

4. Monitoring Performance Post-Deployment

4.1 Real-Time Monitoring

After deployment, monitoring application performance in real time is essential for identifying potential issues quickly.

4.1.1 Application Insights

As mentioned earlier, Azure Application Insights provides real-time monitoring capabilities, including:

- **Request Tracking**: Monitor response times, request rates, and failure rates to identify performance bottlenecks.
- **Dependency Tracking**: Analyze the performance of external dependen-

cies (e.g., databases, APIs).

- **Live Metrics Stream**: View real-time metrics to diagnose issues as they arise.

4.2 User Experience Monitoring

Monitoring user interactions with the application provides insights into how performance affects the user experience.

4.2.1 Session Tracking

Track user sessions to understand how users navigate through the application and identify areas where performance issues may arise.

4.2.2 Error Tracking

Monitor and log errors to identify patterns or recurring issues that may impact user experience.

```csharp
Copy code
_logger.LogError(exception, "An error occurred while processing
request for user {UserId}", userId);
```

4.3 Performance Metrics Analysis

Regularly analyze performance metrics to gain insights into application health and identify areas for optimization.

4.3.1 Key Performance Indicators (KPIs)

Define and track KPIs that align with business goals, such as:

- **Response Time**: Average time taken to process user requests.
- **Throughput**: Number of requests processed per minute.
- **Error Rate**: Percentage of requests that result in errors.

4.4 Incident Response

Implement an incident response plan to address performance issues quickly. Key steps include:

- **Detection**: Use monitoring tools to detect anomalies in performance metrics.
- **Investigation**: Analyze logs and metrics to determine the root cause of performance issues.
- **Resolution**: Implement fixes or optimizations based on the findings of the investigation.

5. Managing Configuration and Secrets

5.1 Configuration Management

Effective configuration management is critical for ensuring that applications behave as expected in different environments.

5.1.1 Environment-Specific Configurations

Use environment-specific configuration files and environment variables to manage settings across different stages of the application lifecycle.

5.1.2 Azure App Configuration

Azure App Configuration provides a centralized way to manage application settings and feature flags.

- **Centralized Management**: Store configuration settings in Azure and retrieve them at runtime, allowing for easy updates without redeploying the application.

5.2 Secrets Management

Managing sensitive information, such as API keys and connection strings, is essential for securing applications.

5.2.1 Azure Key Vault

Azure Key Vault is a secure service for storing and managing secrets, keys, and certificates.

- **Secure Storage**: Store sensitive information securely and retrieve it programmatically in your application.
- **Access Control**: Use Azure Active Directory (AAD) to control access to secrets based on user roles.

5.3 Configuration Refresh

Implement a strategy for refreshing configuration settings at runtime to ensure that changes are applied without requiring a redeployment.

5.3.1 Implementing Configuration Refresh

Use the IOptionsSnapshot<T> interface to reload configuration settings when they change.

```csharp
Copy code
public class MyService
{
    private readonly IOptionsSnapshot<MyOptions> _options;

    public MyService(IOptionsSnapshot<MyOptions> options)
    {
        _options = options;
    }

    public void DoSomething()
    {
        var currentSettings = _options.Value;
```

```
        // Use currentSettings
    }
}
```

6. Rollback Strategies

6.1 Importance of Rollback Plans

Despite thorough testing and monitoring, deployments can sometimes encounter unexpected issues. Having a rollback plan is essential for quickly reverting to a previous stable version.

6.2 Implementing Rollback Procedures

Establish clear rollback procedures as part of the deployment process:

6.2.1 Automated Rollback

Use automated rollback mechanisms in your deployment pipeline to revert to a previous version if issues are detected after deployment.

6.2.2 Manual Rollback

Ensure that deployment teams have the necessary tools and procedures in place for manual rollback if automated methods fail.

6.3 Testing Rollback Procedures

Regularly test rollback procedures to ensure that they can be executed quickly and effectively in a production environment.

7. Conclusion

Deploying high-performance applications in .NET 6 requires careful planning, effective strategies, and adherence to best practices. By understanding the deployment process, leveraging cloud services, and implementing robust monitoring and rollback capabilities, organizations can ensure that their applications perform optimally while minimizing risks associated with deployment.

This chapter explored various aspects of application deployment, including deployment strategies such as blue-green, rolling, and canary deployments. We also discussed the importance of monitoring performance post-deployment, managing configuration and secrets, and implementing rollback strategies.

As technology continues to evolve and user expectations rise, organizations must remain agile and proactive in their deployment practices. By embracing continuous integration and continuous deployment (CI/CD) and prioritizing performance and reliability, developers can deliver high-quality applications that meet the demands of users while adapting to the challenges of an ever-changing landscape.

In summary, effective deployment practices are crucial for the success of high-performance applications. By leveraging the capabilities of .NET 6 and cloud services, organizations can create scalable, reliable, and high-performance applications that provide exceptional user experiences and meet the evolving needs of their customers.

Conclusion: Mastering High-Performance Applications with .NET 6

As the digital landscape continues to evolve at an unprecedented pace, the demand for high-performance applications has never been greater. Organizations are increasingly recognizing that user experience, scalability, and security are paramount in developing software that meets modern expectations. Throughout this book, we have explored the multifaceted approach required to design, build, and maintain high-performance applications using .NET 6. In this conclusion, we will summarize the key takeaways from each chapter, highlighting the essential components of building robust, efficient, and scalable applications.

1. The Role of .NET 6 in High-Performance Computing

The introduction of .NET 6 has significantly advanced the capabilities of the .NET ecosystem, providing developers with enhanced performance features, cross-platform support, and a modern programming model. The unification of .NET frameworks under .NET 6 allows developers to build applications that are not only performant but also easier to maintain and scale. The focus on performance improvements, such as faster startup times, reduced memory footprint, and enhanced garbage collection, sets the stage for building applications capable of meeting the demands of modern workloads.

1.1 Key Features of .NET 6

- **Cross-Platform Development**: .NET 6 allows developers to build applications that run seamlessly on Windows, macOS, and Linux, broadening the deployment options.
- **Performance Optimizations**: Significant enhancements in JIT compilation, garbage collection, and libraries ensure that applications run faster and more efficiently.
- **Unified Platform**: The unification of .NET Core and .NET Framework under a single platform simplifies the development process and improves developer productivity.

2. Architecture and Design Principles

The architecture and design principles laid out in the earlier chapters serve as the foundation for building high-performance applications. By adopting scalable architectures, such as microservices and event-driven designs, developers can create systems that are both flexible and resilient.

2.1 Scalability Considerations

Understanding scalability is crucial for ensuring that applications can grow with user demand. By implementing design patterns like microservices and serverless architecture, organizations can optimize resource usage and improve fault tolerance. The ability to scale horizontally allows for effective load distribution, ensuring that applications remain responsive under varying conditions.

2.2 Design Patterns and Best Practices

Design patterns, such as the repository and unit of work patterns, facilitate maintainable and testable code. Best practices for secure coding, data validation, and adherence to the principle of least privilege further enhance application reliability. By embedding security considerations into the application lifecycle, developers can mitigate risks associated with data breaches and compliance violations.

3. Performance Optimization Techniques

Performance optimization is an ongoing process that requires continuous monitoring, testing, and refinement. The techniques discussed throughout this book provide developers with the tools they need to identify bottlenecks and improve application performance.

3.1 Memory Management

Effective memory management techniques, including the use of Span<T> and object pooling, can significantly reduce garbage collection overhead and enhance performance. By understanding the nuances of memory allocation and optimizing memory usage, developers can create applications that respond more quickly to user interactions.

3.2 Asynchronous Programming

The adoption of asynchronous programming patterns in .NET 6 allows developers to write non-blocking code that maximizes resource utilization. By leveraging the async and await keywords, applications can handle multiple concurrent operations without sacrificing responsiveness. This is particularly important for I/O-bound tasks, where traditional synchronous programming would lead to resource contention.

4. Security and Compliance

Data security and compliance are critical components of any modern application. As organizations face increasing scrutiny regarding data privacy, it is essential to implement robust security measures that protect sensitive information while ensuring compliance with regulations.

4.1 Secure Coding Practices

By adhering to secure coding practices and leveraging built-in security features in .NET 6, developers can minimize vulnerabilities. This includes input validation, proper authentication and authorization mechanisms, and the use of encryption for data protection. Implementing role-based and policy-based authorization ensures that access control is both flexible and secure.

4.2 Compliance Regulations

Organizations must navigate various compliance regulations, such as GDPR, HIPAA, and PCI DSS, which dictate how data should be handled and protected. Understanding the implications of these regulations is crucial for building applications that adhere to legal requirements and avoid costly penalties. By integrating compliance considerations into the development process, organizations can mitigate risks and build trust with users.

5. Deployment and Maintenance

Deployment practices have a direct impact on application performance and user experience. By adopting best practices for deployment and maintenance, organizations can ensure smooth transitions from development to production and maintain application health over time.

5.1 Deployment Strategies

Understanding various deployment strategies, such as blue-green, rolling, and canary deployments, allows organizations to minimize downtime and reduce the risk of introducing errors into production environments. Automated deployment pipelines, coupled with CI/CD practices, facilitate rapid and reliable releases.

5.2 Monitoring and Performance Management

Post-deployment monitoring is essential for identifying performance issues and ensuring that applications continue to meet user expectations. Utilizing tools like Azure Application Insights and other monitoring solutions enables developers to gain real-time insights into application performance, user interactions, and system health. By analyzing performance metrics and user feedback, organizations can continuously optimize their applications for better performance.

6. Future Considerations

As technology continues to evolve, the landscape of application development will also change. Emerging trends such as artificial intelligence, machine learning, and edge computing will shape the future of high-performance applications. Developers must remain agile and open to adopting new tools, frameworks, and methodologies that enhance their ability to deliver scalable and performant software.

6.1 Embracing New Technologies

Staying informed about advancements in technology, such as container orchestration (e.g., Kubernetes), serverless architectures, and AI-driven optimization tools, will empower developers to leverage these innovations in their applications. This adaptability will be key to maintaining competitiveness in an increasingly complex digital environment.

6.2 Continuous Learning and Improvement

Fostering a culture of continuous learning within development teams encourages the exploration of new technologies and methodologies. Regular training sessions, workshops, and knowledge-sharing initiatives can help developers stay current with industry trends and best practices. This commitment to growth will lead to better-informed decision-making and improved application quality.

Conclusion

In conclusion, mastering high-performance application development with .NET 6 requires a comprehensive understanding of architecture, design principles, performance optimization, security, compliance, and deployment practices. By integrating these elements into the development process, organizations can build applications that not only perform exceptionally well but also meet the rigorous demands of modern users.

Throughout this book, we have explored the various dimensions of building high-performance applications in .NET 6, emphasizing the importance of a holistic approach. By leveraging the capabilities of .NET 6, embracing best practices, and remaining adaptable to changing technologies, developers can create resilient, scalable, and secure applications that deliver value to users and stakeholders alike.

As the digital landscape continues to evolve, the journey toward high-performance application development is ongoing. By prioritizing performance, security, and user experience, organizations can position themselves for success in an increasingly competitive environment, paving the way for innovation and growth in the future.